T0295727

Trade and Investment in South Asia

An Analysis

Trade and Investment in South Asia

An Analysis

Rahul Choudhury
National University of Singapore

Dinkar Nayak
Maharaja Sayajirao University of Baroda, India

NEW JERSEY · LONDON · SINGAPORE · BEIJING · SHANGHAI · HONG KONG · TAIPEI · CHENNAI · TOKYO

Published by

World Scientific Publishing Co. Pte. Ltd.

5 Toh Tuck Link, Singapore 596224

USA office: 27 Warren Street, Suite 401-402, Hackensack, NJ 07601

UK office: 57 Shelton Street, Covent Garden, London WC2H 9HE

Library of Congress Cataloging-in-Publication Data
Names: Choudhury, Rahul Nath, author. | Nayak, Dinkar, author.
Title: Trade and investment in South Asia : an analysis / Rahul Choudhury (National University
    of Singapore, Singapore), Dinkar Nayak (Maharaja Sayajirao University of Baroda, India).
Description: 1 Edition. | New Jersey : World Scientific, [2019] |
    Includes bibliographical references and index.
Identifiers: LCCN 2019020533 | ISBN 9789811206566
Subjects: LCSH: Investments, Foreign--South Asia. | South Asia--Commerce. |
    South Asian cooperation.
Classification: LCC HG5720.3.A3 C46 2019 | DDC 330.954--dc23
LC record available at https://lccn.loc.gov/2019020533

British Library Cataloguing-in-Publication Data
A catalogue record for this book is available from the British Library.

For any available supplementary material, please visit
https://www.worldscientific.com/worldscibooks/10.1142/11450#t=suppl

Desk Editor: Shreya Gopi

Typeset by Stallion Press
Email: enquiries@stallionpress.com

Contents

Foreword

Even in this era of universal connectivity and global digitalisation, South Asia remains one of the least integrated regions in the world. Furthermore, the amount of Foreign Direct Investment (FDI) remains woefully minimal. Moreover, 90% of the quantum is concentrated in India. The intra-regional investment scenario is also poor. Trade within the region accounts for less than 10% of the region's global trade.

The countries of South Asia have so far failed to take advantage of the complementarity that exists among themselves, which otherwise could have paved the path for more economic activities through burgeoning synergies. This is despite the fact that several South Asian countries share common borders. Within India, the regions close to Nepal, Bhutan, and Bangladesh experience lower growth as compared to the rest of the economy. Cross-border trade continues to remain considerably below potential. The high volume of informal trade further reduces the trade volume through legal channels. Despite the existence of the South Asian Free Trade Area (SAFTA), trading with neighbours is far from being free. This is mainly due to the long list of products that are not included under the concessional tariff of SAFTA.

FDI inflows and its potential role in economic growth is a well-researched subject. Inter-State investment, intra-regional tourism, and knowledge sharing are well below their potential. Several studies conducted on this topic have attempted to explore various aspects of the phenomenon. In spite of that, there still exists a wide gap in extant literature. This book endeavours to bridge the gap.

This book attempts to discern the prevailing investment scenario and possible constraints in augmenting trade-investment linkages in South Asia. It also seeks to examine investment potentials and opportunities in several sectors. Analyses of the existing FDI policies of select countries, the extent of flow of technology and management ideas through FDI, and the integration of production activities across the borders are well documented by the authors. The book offers an elaborative explanation of the impact of FDI inflows and outflows on investing as well as receiving economies. The ranking of individual countries of South Asia in the Ease of Doing Business Index has been thoroughly explained along with measures to elevate the respective positions. The authors have also undertaken a meticulous investigation with regard to the relationship between trade and investment in individual countries in the region.

I sincerely believe that this book will be an invaluable addition to the existing literature on trade and investment relations. It promises to be of major benefit to readers with a general interest in this topic. Policy makers will also profit from in-depth research on regional trade and investment scenarios. I am confident that this book will greatly serve as a ready reference for students, academics, researchers, and policymakers. Plaudits are owed to the authors, Dr Rahul Nath Choudhury and Dr Dinkar Nayak for their efforts in producing this comprehensive volume and offering such an in-depth analysis of a topic of such immense importance. It is my hope that the authors will continue to work on the many and varied aspects of trade and investment relationship in South Asia. I would wish them every success in their future efforts, including contributions to the study and examination of these and related issues to the benefit of all concerned.

Dr. Iftekhar Ahmed Chowdhury
(Former Foreign Minister of Bangladesh)
Principal Research Fellow; and Research Lead
Institute of South Asian Studies
National University of Singapore
Singapore

List of Abbreviations

AAGR	Average Annual Growth Rate
ADF	Augmented Dickey Fuller
ASEAN	Association for South East Asian Countries
BF	Business Freedom
BIPA	Bilateral Investment Protection Agreement
BOI	Board of Investment
BoT	Balance of Trade
BPO	Business Process Outsourcing
CIF	Cost Insurance Freight
CBA	Collective Bargaining Agents
CUSUMSQ	Cumulative Sum Square
DGPC	Druk Green Power Corporation
DIPP	Department of Industrial Policy and Promotion
DIN	Domestic Investment
DTAA	Double Taxation Avoidance Agreement
EU	European Union
FDI	Foreign Direct Investment
FE	Fixed Effect
FERA	Foreign Exchange Regulatory Act
FF	Fiscal Freedom
FITTA	Foreign Investment and Technology Act
FoB	Free on Board
GDP	Gross Domestic Product
GF	Governance Freedom

GNH	Gross National Happiness
GNP	Gross National Product
GST	Goods and Service Tax
HS	Harmonized System
IEA	Industrial Enterprise Act
IF	Investment Freedom
IIP	Index of Industrial Production
IMF	International Monetary Fund
IPR	Intellectual Property Right
LDC	Least Developed Countries
LM test	Lagrange Multiplier
LSDV	Least Square Dummy Variable
MENA	Middle East and North Africa region
MNC	Multinational Company
MNE	Multinational Enterprises
NR	Nepalese Rupee
NTB	Non-Tariff barriers
Nu	Ngultrum
OLS	Ordinary Least Square
PAN	Permanent Account Number
PPP	Purchasing Power Parity
PVC	Polyvinyl chloride
R&D	Research & Development
RBOB	Royal Bank of Bhutan
RE	Random Effect
RMG	Ready-Made Garments
RTA	Regional Trade Agreement
SAARC	South Asian Association for Regional Co-operation
SAP	Structural Adjustment Programme
SAPTA	South Asian Preferential Trade Agreement
SIA	Secretariat for Industrial Assistance
SUR	Seemingly Unrelated Regressions
TAN	Tax Account Number
TF	Trade Freedom
TWMNC	Third World Multinational Corporations

UAE	United Arab Emirate
UK	United Kingdom
UN	United Nations
UNCTAD	United Nations Conference on Trade and Development
USA	United States of America
VAR	Vector Auto Regression
WITS	World Integrated Trade Solution
WTO	World Trade Organization

Acknowledgments

The passion to explore the unexplored is what drives one's spirit toward excellence. The journey — though challenging at times — is the most rewarding experience. However, to reach the desired destination, our determination must align with a dedication to getting in the right direction. Having said this, during the course of our journey, there were times when we felt exhausted; sometimes, we even thought of quitting before reaching the destination. But, with the support of and encouragement from friends and well-wishers, we continued to tread along this path with total dedication. Writing this book has been enlightening and a wonderful intellectual experience. Now that we have accomplished our goal, we would like to take this opportunity to convey our sincere gratitude to all those who have contributed in numerous ways to give a final shape to our book.

This book is an updated and substantially revised version of the PhD thesis entitled "A Comparative Study of Investment Flows in SAARC Countries: An Analysis" submitted by Rahul Nath Choudhury under the supervision of Dr. Dinkar Nayak, in 2014 at the Department of Business Economics, Faculty of Commerce, The Maharaja Sayajirao University of Baroda, Vadodara, Gujarat, India.

First and foremost, we would like to express our gratitude to the Institute of South Asian Studies (ISAS) at the National University of Singapore for giving us the opportunity to write this book. We are indebted to Mr. Gopinath Pillai, Chairman of ISAS and Ambassador-at-Large at the Ministry of Foreign Affairs, Singapore, for his support and best wishes.

We are thankful to Dr. Subrata Kumar Mitra, former Director, ISAS, for believing in us and encouraging us to write this book. Gratitude is due to Dr. C Raja Mohan, Director of ISAS for his support and encouragement.

We are grateful to Mr. Hernaikh Singh, Associate Director, ISAS, for his constant support and providing us with an environment to pursue and reach our goal.

We would like to express our deep gratitude to Dr. Amitendu Palit, Senior Research Fellow and Research Lead at ISAS for his constant encouragement and intellectual support to take the work forward. Discussions with him on various occasions about this project have been of great help.

We extend our special thanks to Dr. Rijesh R. The book has immensely benefitted from the discussions held with him during the various stages of the study, especially during the analysis of the data. His comments have helped us to improve the study to a large extent. We are grateful for his cooperation and contribution.

We take this opportunity to thank our friend Pravin Jadhav for helping us collect and analyze the data. Our discussions with regard to the study of literature have helped us acquire an in-depth knowledge of the subject.

We are thankful to all staff members at ISAS for their good wishes.

We are sincerely thankful to Ms. Shreya Gopi, Editor at the World Scientific and the anonymous reviewers for keeping their faith on us since the proposal stage and pushing us to complete the task.

A special "thank you" goes to our wonderful families for their encouragement and cooperation through the years.

Last but not least, we would like to thank the Almighty for His immense blessings and the strength provided not only to undertake this journey, but also to complete it.

Rahul Nath Choudhury
Dinkar Nayak

Chapter 1

Introduction

All member countries of SAARC follow an open and liberal trade and investment policy. The SAARC region has attracted a sizable volume of foreign investment from various parts of the world and also emerged as a significant player in global trade in the very recent period. It is in this connection that this book examines the relationship between trade and foreign direct investment in the SAARC region. This book also explores the intra-regional flow of trade and investment in the SAARC region. Further, it also investigates the role of the government policies responsible for attracting foreign investment and increasing the volume of the trade.

1.1. Introduction

Have you ever wondered why cross-country investment flows in the form of foreign direct investment (FDI) was considered as an alternative form of international capital? Truth be told, preceding 1950, FDI was viewed as a subset of portfolio investment (Kindleberger, 1969). It was in the 1960s that an appropriate clarification of FDI was sought, when academicians attempted to incorporate the exercises of multinational corporations (MNCs) with the theories of FDI (Rayome & Baker, 1995). It was proposed that the endeavors made by different nations to draw in FDI are because of the potential constructive outcomes related to remote speculation, which prompts monetary advancement in the host nation. It was enunciated that FDI would build profitability, get new innovation exchange, bring in administrative aptitudes and know-how, and create global systems, which would increase employment opportunities and provide access to the external market, thereby expanding trade (Caves, 1996). It was additionally stated that FDI prompts an overflow of cutting-edge innovations to neighborhood firms (Findlay, 1978). Considering this, numerous countries through the years have endeavored to facilitate expanded streams of inward FDI. It is in this setting that the South Asian Association for Regional Co-operation (SAARC) nations have made different endeavors to draw in FDI.

Earlier, majority of the SAARC nations had been following import-substitution-driven development in accordance with the overall reasoning of the 1950s. But in the mid-1970s, the limitation of inward-looking growth model became apparent. In a similar manner, Sri Lanka started export-promotion-led economic reforms in the late 1970s. Bangladesh experienced an International Monetary Fund (IMF)-endorsed Structural Adjustment Program (SAP) in the mid-1980s, while India encountered a comparable change about 10 years after the Bangladesh development. Likewise, Nepal attempted financial strategy changes in mid-1990s. A remarkable track in this change procedure was the advancement of the outside division. Given the issue of surplus work and capital shortage faced by all South Asian nations to varying degrees, it was felt that the monetary change process won't just expand the stream of FDI yet. In addition, that would lead to extension exchange and accordingly advance financial development and improvement. Further, the existing empirical literature indicates that regional integration arrangements considerably reduce trade costs among partner countries, which not only augment trade but also acts as a stimulus to FDI flow. It is widely accepted that trade and investment together function as a major catalyst for economic development when accompanied by favorable domestic policy.

FDI has always been an exciting enterprise for academicians. Numerous scholars, within the established and existing domains in the fields of trade and investment, have defined and analyzed FDI, providing significant insights into various disciplines. So far, many scholars have covered the following issues extensively.

One of the first studies that has examined the effect of FDI on growth was conducted by Lall and Streeten (1977). They examined 88 foreign-owned and locally owned projects in six different countries using cost–benefit analysis to estimate the national income effect of FDI. In their analysis, they came to the conclusion that the effect of FDI on national income was positive for about 58 countries and negative for the remaining 30 countries. In a similar research conducted by Encarnation and Ethier (1986), the contribution of 50 FDI projects made to national income minus cost to the national economy, both at the world prices, was calculated. They found that the majority of the projects would not increase the national income, while the remaining sizable minority would actually decrease the country's national income.

Blomstrom, Lipsey and Zejan (1994) analyzed the data for 78 developing and 23 developed countries. They found that the inflow of FDI had a significant positive influence on the income growth rate of the host countries. The influence was mainly confined to those developing countries having a higher level of income. However, the same trend was not evident among poor countries. They, therefore, concluded that the host countries will benefit from the investment of foreign firms if they had a certain threshold level of development.

Fry (1993) analyzed the effects of FDI in a macroeconomic framework consisting of investment, saving, growth, and current account equations. He applied this framework to a sample of 16 developing countries including India. From his analysis, he found that for 11 developing countries, FDI is associated with the reduced domestic investment. This implies that for these countries FDI is simply a close substitute for other capital inflows. But for the remaining five countries, FDI was found to raise domestic investment. In other words, the impact of FDI on growth shows a mixed result. However, Chen *et al.* (1995), using time series data for the period 1979–1993, found that there exists a positive relationship between FDI and gross national product (GNP) for the Chinese economy. Their result was also significant at a 5% level.

In another research paper by Balasubramanyam, Salisu and Sapsford (1996), the hypothesis of Bhagwati (1978) that export-led growth strategy can reap enormous benefits from FDI was tested. By employing the CUSUMSQ test, the Bhagwati hypothesis was tested with the help of cross-section data for 46 countries for the period 1970–1975.[1] From their analysis, they concluded that FDI provides a fillip to the process of economic growth to those countries pursuing an outward policy.

Barrell and Pain (1996) put forward the argument that FDI could enhance growth in the host economy. They used the panel data method to conclude that FDI in European countries has led to a higher GDP growth by increasing exports.

Blomstrom and Kokko (1997) examined the host country effect of FDI. They mainly focused on the transfer and diffusion of technology from an MNC to the host country and examined the impact of MNC on the trade performance of the host country. They concluded that FDI may promote development by enhancing productivity growth and export from the host country. However, the impact varies from industry to industry and country to country. In other words, the net benefit of FDI deepens the host country's industry and policy environment.

A similar research was conducted by Dutt (1997) to investigate the impact of sectoral FDI inflows and economic growth.[2] He tested the hypothesis proposed by Singer (1950).[3] On the basis of Singers'

---

[1] Cumulative sum squared (CUSUSMQ) tests is used to test the constancy of the coefficients in a model. See Brown Durbin and Evans (1975).

[2] However, UNCTAD (2007) identified several channels through which FDI in primary sector can help the host countries to exploit the natural resources in such a way that it provides an opportunity for development and growth. The channels are in the form of provision of financial resources, transfer of technology, and provide necessary skills with the help of which technology barriers can be worked out.

[3] Singer has stressed that FDI in developing countries mainly goes to the primary sector rather than the manufacturing sector. He argued that due to low-income elasticity of demand of primary product, the benefit of FDI will go more to the consumer in the form of lower prices rather than to the producer in the form of higher profit.

hypothesis, Dutt (1997) argued that FDI in the manufacturing sector will have a more positive implication for the host developing country because of greater technological development of this sector, whereas primary FDI may not have a positive effect due to the less technologically advanced product produced by the sector. However, by using cross-country growth equation and data of 47 countries for the period 1985–1994, Dutt did not find any empirical support for his argument. In other words, FDI in both primary and manufacturing sector appears insignificant in his analysis.

Borensztein, De Gregorio and Lee (1998), on the basis of the endogenous growth model, tested the effect of FDI on economic growth of 69 developing countries for two different time periods: 1970–1979 and 1980–1989. From their analysis, they came to the conclusion that the effect of FDI on economic growth depends upon the level of human capital development in the host country. The authors found that the impact is greater for those countries having a high level of human capital development. Further, the contribution of FDI to growth is relatively higher as compared to domestic investment.

Another research work that has examined the sector-wise impact of FDI was conducted by Alfaro (2003). The author argued that the impact of FDI on the economic growth of host countries varies across primary, manufacturing, and service sectors. The benefits of FDI, such as transfer of production technology, innovation, organizational and managerial skills, and the ability to enter the international markets, are more likely to occur for manufacturing FDI rather than primary FDI. This is because the linkages between foreign and domestic firms are generally weak in agriculture and mining sectors, which curb the impact of primary FDI on economic growth in the host country.

Hansen and Rand (2006) have analyzed the relationships between FDI and GDP with a sample of 31 developing countries covering three continents for a 30-year time period between 1970 and 2000. The authors employed the Granger causality test. It was found in the research that there is a strong causal link between GDP and FDI. In the long run, when allowing for country's specific heterogeneity of all parameters, it was found that FDI has a significant long-run impact on countries during the period's GDP irrespective of the level of development. Thus, as per their analysis, no significant difference across regions was found.

Adewumi (2007) analyzed the impact of FDI inflows on the economic growth of developing countries considering the case of select African countries for the time period of 1970–2003. He found that the contribution was positive from the overall continent's point of view. But in terms of selected countries, it was discovered that effect is positive for some cases and not positive in others. Further, in most of the countries and for the continent as a whole, the relevant coefficient estimate is not significant. It was pointed out by the author that the negative result obtained may be due to relatively low FDI flows to the African countries.

Johnson (2006) also examined the effect of FDI inflows on a host country's economic growth both for developing as well as developed economies. The paper argued that FDI should have a positive impact on economic growth due to technological spillover and inflow of physical capital. With the help of both cross-section and panel data analysis covering 1980–2002, the paper indicated that FDI enhances economic growth in developing countries but not in a developed country. This may be reflected in a developed market economy where there is no difference between domestic and international investment.

Mengistu and Adams (2007) explored how the inflow of FDI affects the domestic investment scenario and economic growth in the host country. The analysis employed cross-section data of 88 developing countries to empirically investigate the issue. Using ordinary least squares (OLS) method and fixed effect estimation techniques, the authors observed the existence of significant correlation between FDI and economic growth. It was found that FDI had a greater impact on Asian countries than on other developing countries. The results also showed a co-relation between institutional infrastructure and economic growth of the host economy.

Beugelsdijk, Smeets and Zwinkels (2008) have explored the impact of US MNCs on the economic growth of host countries by making a distinction between the broad effects of horizontal FDI and vertical FDI.[4] The authors used panel data for a time period of 20 years from 1983 to 2003 and a sample of 44 host countries. The results suggest that both horizontal FDI and vertical FDI have a positive and significant effect in developed countries. The growth effect of horizontal FDI is about 50% larger than the vertical FDI in this set of developed countries. The paper finds no significant relationship between horizontal FDI and vertical FDI and growth in developing countries.

Recent studies come to the conclusion that FDI varies from one country to another depending upon whether the local factors are conducive to FDI inflows. For instance, Ali (2010) found that the impact of FDI on economic growth depends upon the institutional quality of the host country. On the basis of a sample of 62 countries including 40 developing countries,[5] he found that those countries that have acquired the minimum threshold of institutional quality have benefited even from primary FDI. The implication of this result is that policymakers should direct their efforts in improving institutional quality to reap the benefits of FDI.

Another work by Djurovic (2011) analyzed the impact of FDI inflows to the economic growth for all developing countries for the period from 2000 to 2010. He used the endogenous model for the analysis. His research model offered a strong inward validity of the impact of FDI on the economic growth of the developing countries in the past decades. The findings indicate that FDI was more attractive for developing countries with higher availability of educated labor, higher government spending, and efficient governance.

Farkas (2012) examined the impact of FDI on economic growth on the basis of the absorptive capacities of the host country covering the period between 1975 and 2000. The cross-section data for 69 countries were used for the research. He found the contribution of FDI

---

[4]In horizontal FDI, multiplant firms duplicate the same activities in multiple countries, while in vertical FDI, firms locate different stages of production in different countries.

[5]India was also included in the sample.

to economic growth was positive and significant. Further, the results indicated that a minimum level of human capital and well-developed financial market are necessary for a positive impact from FDI.

The main conclusion from the aforementioned surveys is that there seems to be a strong relationship between FDI and economic growth. But at the same time, there are studies that point to a weak relationship between development and FDI. Thus, the results are mixed. Some research works concluded that the contribution of FDI to growth is positive, but it depends on some factors in the host country such as the sector to which the FDI flows, the human capital base of the country, and the degree of openness in the country. It is also noteworthy that some studies have claimed that the contribution of FDI to growth is not positive.

1.2. Impact of FDI in the SAARC Region

One of the pioneering works on FDI in the SAARC region was conducted by Sengupta and Banik (1997).[6] The authors argued that FDI and regional trade are generally mutually supportive. According to the authors, FDI as a fraction of GDP is marginal among all the SAARC countries. Yet it was found that there is a significant positive impact of FDI on gross national investment of the member countries with exception of Nepal, India when measured individually. Measuring gross national investment collectively for the entire SAARC region, however, gives us a negative result. The authors were of the view that benefits to the host country will depend on both the size of the package of incentives and disincentives to FDI, and the extent of other distortions in the economy. As far as the impact of FDI on export was concerned, it was found to be positive in the SAARC countries with the exception of the Maldives. FDI inflows in the reference period raised exports and reduced imports from non-SAARC and SAARC countries.

Agrawal (2000), in his research work, provided the empirical evidence for the positive association between FDI, national investment, and economic growth. The author used time series cross-section

---

[6] The paper included all the eight member countries of the SAARC region.

panel data from five major South Asian countries covering the time period between 1965 and 1996 to estimate the impact of FDI inflows on domestic investment and on GDP growth.[7] He argued that there exists a complementary linkage between foreign and national investment. Agrawal found that the impact of FDI on GDP growth was negative before the 1980s, but the reverse was noticed in late 1980s and early 1990s. They supported the argument that FDI is more likely to be beneficial in more open economies.

Sahoo (2006) made an extensive investigation about the policy, trends, impact, and determinants of FDI in the SAARC region. The author employed panel co-integration method for the analysis for the period of 1970–2003. He found all the five South Asian countries were lacking in adequate infrastructure facilities and governance.[8] The FDI in South Asia is mostly concentrated in the manufacturing and service sectors. For Indian and Pakistan, FDI inflows were found to be dominating the domestic market, whereas for Sri Lanka and Bangladesh it is found to be in the export market-oriented sector. The analysis found a positive impact of FDI on the economic growth of South Asian countries. However, Pakistan was an exception in this regard. Sahoo (2006) also pointed out market size, labor force growth, infrastructure index, and trade openness as major determinants of FDI in the South Asian region.

Iftikhar (2012) analyzed the relationship between FDI and economic growth in select SAARC countries for the period 1970–2004. The author employed heterogeneous panel co-integration technique and Granger causality test. He found a strong causal link between FDI and GDP. His findings indicate that as FDI promotes growth, GDP growth also helps attract more FDI inflows. Once domestic growth is enhanced and stimulated, further foreign investment would come in. The result of the analysis suggested that the economic growth of the SAARC region can further be promoted by FDI inflows in the region. The SAARC countries may benefit from

---

[7] India, Pakistan, Bangladesh, Sri Lanka, and Nepal.
[8] The paper includes only five South Asian countries: India, Pakistan, Nepal, Sri Lanka, and Bangladesh.

adopting investment-friendly policies that attract FDI flows into their economies.

Javed *et al.* (2012) explored the relationship among FDI, imports, exports, domestic investment, and economic growth in four South Asian countries.[9] The analysis used time series (annual) data for the time period between 1973 and 2010. The authors employed the Granger causality test to analyze the relationship between the variables. On the basis of the test results, the authors argued that imports are caused by GDP at different lag periods in all the selected countries. But no evidence of causality from imports to GDP was found in the research. The authors also argued in support of the two-way causality between FDI and trade openness. The authors have also supported the adoption of liberal policies to increase investment in the host country.

1.3. Studies Related to Individual SAARC Member Countries

1.3.1. *Pakistan*

Atique *et al.* (2004) argued that the impact of FDI on economic growth of Pakistan tends to be greater under an export promotion trade regime as compared to an import-substitution regime. The research paper employed time series data for Pakistan for the period 1970–2001. The analysis pointed out the trade policy regime as one of the major factors of growth associated with Transnational Corporation (TNC) and FDI inflow. The authors argued that FDI can stimulate human resource development through investment in education and training. This will further enhance the stock of human capital and also increase the productivity of labor and other factors of production.

Yousaf (2008) argued that FDI has contributed significantly to the development of human resources, capital formation and improvement of organizational and managerial skills in Pakistan. The authors analyzed the impact of FDI on imports and exports of

---

[9]The paper included only four countries in the South Asian region, namely, Bangladesh, India, Pakistan, and Sri Lanka.

Pakistan using time series data. They employed co-integration techniques for the period between 1973 and 2004. The results suggest that FDI has positively impacted the real demand for imports both in the short and long run. The results also found that with 1% increase in FDI inflow, the real demand for import has increased by 0.08% in the short run, while it increased by 0.52% in the case of a long run. However, with 1% increase in FDI inflow, the real export has decreased by 0.08% in the short run and increased by 1.62% in the long run. The research also mentioned political instability and lack of infrastructural facilities as major hurdles to inflow of FDI.

Falki (2009) investigated the impact of FDI on economic growth of Pakistan during the period of 1980–2006. Falki used a theoretical model developed by Cobb–Douglas and Granger causality technique to examine the relationship between FDI and economic growth. He found a negative and statistically insignificant relationship between the GDP and FDI inflows in Pakistan in his reference period. The author argued that liberal trade regime, a threshold level of endowments of human capital and an adequate domestic market for the goods produced are some of the preconditions for attracting FDI. The results suggested that the government should formulate policy variables in such a way so that it can attract more investment.

Yousaf *et al.* (2011) found FDI has a negative impact on the economic growth of Pakistan during the period of 1980–2009. They used the OLS model for empirical analysis. The results reported unfavorable government policy, technological gap and underqualified human skills have been the major hurdle in exploiting the benefits of FDI. The results suggest that the government should create opportunities for the foreign investors to transfer current management skills and technological innovations and provide sound business environment and opportunities to strengthen the local markets.

Tabassum, Nazeer and Siddiqui (2012) analyzed the relationship between FDI with both import demand and export supply of Pakistan. The analysis covered the time period from 1973 to 2009. The author employed co-integration method for the analysis. The results argued that FDI generally has a tendency to increase the host country's imports because MNCs often have a high tendency to import intermediate inputs, capital goods, and services. The results showed that there exists a stable and long-run equilibrium relationship between real import and FDI. The author also found a positive and long-run relationship between FDI and real exports in Pakistan.

1.3.2. *Sri Lanka*

Athukorala (2003) used time series data from 1959 to 2002 to assess the impact of FDI on economic growth of Sri Lanka. The author applied the co-integration model to capture the two-way linkage between FDI and trade. He argued that attractive investment opportunities are available for foreign companies in Sri Lanka. He also argued that a number of policy measures have been initiated by the Sri Lankan government to attract international investment into the country. Sri Lanka also offers one of the most liberal FDI regimes in South Asia. Lack of transparency in trade policy, discrimination against non-export-oriented sectors and high lending rate were found to be the major constraints to FDI flows in Sri Lanka. The analysis suggested developing of the port network, road and rail network, communication facilities, and more flexible labor markets to increase in the inflow of international investment.

Balamurali and Bogahawatte (2004) have investigated the relationship between FDI and economic growth of Sri Lanka over the period 1977–2003. They employed a Granger causality test for the analysis. They found that FDI was a key determinant for Sri Lanka's economic growth after 1977. The authors also found a bidirectional causality between FDI and economic growth in Sri Lanka. The results showed that FDI exerts an independent influence on the economic growth of Sri Lanka. The paper also explored a long-run equilibrium relationship between GDP, FDI, domestic investment (DIN), and openness of trade policy.

1.3.3. *Bangladesh*

Ahamed and Tanin (2010) analyzed the determinants and the relationship between FDI and economic growth in Bangladesh. The analysis covered the time period 1975–2006 and developed multiple regression model based on time series data. They argued that the economic growth of the host country is a significant determinant of FDI. It is the level of economic growth that attracts FDI. The authors argued from the fact that foreign investors invariably prefer to invest not only in large markets but also in economies that are currently experiencing high rates of economic growth. Therefore, the role of FDI is pivotal in providing Bangladesh the necessary finance and capital to achieve sustainable growth as well as poverty alleviation. The authors have also argued that FDI inflows in Bangladesh in recent decades have been able to increase GDP by raising the economy's output capacity and employment level.

Quader (2009) examined the robustness between FDI inflow and various economic indicators and their impact on the Bangladesh economy. A positive relationship was found between FDI and economic growth after examining the time series data for the period of 1990–1991 to 2005–2006. The analysis employed the OLS method and extreme bound method for the analysis and results were found to be significant at 95% level.[10] The results suggested a consistent incentive package should be implemented to encourage foreign investment and to ensure long-term economic growth.

1.3.4. *Nepal*

Athukorala and Sharma (2006) investigated the FDI inflow in Nepal for the period between 1985 and 2001 using time series data. They revealed that in spite of significant liberalization of the economy, foreign investment regime and providing attractive investment incentives, Nepal's achievements in attracting FDI is far from satisfactory levels and national expectations. The paper argued that FDI in Nepal has failed to make a significant contribution to the productivity growth of the manufacturing sector. The authors suggested that Nepal needs to develop the preconditions of investment and trade to enjoy the benefits of FDI.

---

[10] Extreme bounds analysis is a global sensitivity analysis that applies to the choice of variables in a linear regression.

Bista (2010) argued that instability and volatility in the business environment and political instability are the major hurdles in attracting FDI in Nepal. Econometric model based on Cobb–Douglas production function was used for the analysis during the period between 1990 and 2004. The authors argued that the situation in Nepal is such that FDI firms could not behave normally as required for production decision and for smooth trade flow inside and outside the country. Because of growing risk aversion and transaction costs, international firms are not encouraged to invest in Nepal.

1.3.5. *India*

Kumar (2005) examined the effect of FDI on domestic investment in India. He did not find a statistically significant effect of FDI on domestic investment. He argued that the changing policy framework has affected the trends and patterns of FDI inflows in India. The results revealed that India is spending the relatively smaller amounts in the development of technology and R&D. Export-oriented industrialization by India with the FDI has also been much poorer in comparison to other East Asian economies.[11]

Chakraborty and Nunnenkamp (2008) found that FDI inflow has surged in the Indian economy especially after the post-reform period. The Granger causality test was used in the panel co-integration framework for the time series data for the period between 1987 and 2000. The authors argued that FDI stocks and output are co-integrated into the long run. FDI can promote growth through productivity gains resulting from spillovers to local firms. The paper also argued that the impact of output growth in attracting FDI is relatively stronger than that of FDI in inducing economic growth. At the sectoral level, it was found that the favorable growth rate of Indian economy has affected FDI inflows in India. But, it is largely restricted to the manufacturing sector. However, results of Granger causality test revealed that output growth in the services sector has

---

[11] Although a large body of literature on impact of FDI on India's trade and growth is available, in this chapter, recent studies have been reviewed. Other studies will be reviewed in the relevant chapters.

also been stimulated by FDI inflow. Moreover, no causal relationship was found in the primary sector.

Pradhan (2008) found unidirectional causality between FDI and GDP for the Indian economy. The research was conducted for the period 1970–2004. Time series data were used for the analysis. The paper employed Granger causality test to investigate the relationship between FDI inflows and economic growth. He argued economic growth promotes FDI, but FDI does not promote growth. However, the author pointed out that FDI can affect the economy indirectly by productivity spillover and export growth.

Sarode (2012) explored the effect of FDI on capital account and GDP of India. The analysis covered the time period between 1997 and 2011. The authors employed the Granger causality test for the analysis. The author found a negative effect on current account and positive effect on capital account for the period of analysis in India.

From the reviewed research works, it is evident that results again provide a mixed response as far as the impact of FDI on trade and growth is concerned. Some studies have reported a positive impact while some have given evidence that the impact is negative. Further, it is also evident that very few studies have been conducted for all the SAARC member countries. In fact, there is a dearth of research for countries such as Afghanistan, Bhutan, and Maldives. It is this lacuna that this book attempts to bridge.

1.4. Significance of the Current Research

FDI is considered to be one of the very important means for the economic development of a country. The FDI brings modern technology, better managerial skills, and others along with capital into the host country. Better technology and advanced managerial skills stimulate competitiveness in the domestic industry, especially in developing countries. The SAARC region, where all the member countries are developing, have received a huge volume of FDI in the recent times. This large volume of investment has significantly impacted the region. Thus, it is of paramount importance to analyze the role played by FDI in this region as a whole and also at the individual country level. Comparative analysis for each of the member countries is also important in this regard. It is in this context that the present book has the following objectives:

- To examine the existing scenario of trade and investment in the SAARC region;
- To analyze the link between trade and investment in the SAARC region;
- To assess the role of investment policy and other institutional factors in facilitating trade and investment in the region;
- To examine the factors that lead to ease of doing business.

1.5. Chapter Scheme

The entire book has been divided into eight chapters of different lengths. Each chapter deals with different themes in terms of the stated objectives.

Chapter 1 — Introduction

The context and issues are introduced in this chapter. Quite an amount of literature is surveyed here to provide the justification for the current research.

Chapter 2 — Ease and Ruckus of Doing Business in South Asia

There are a number of factors that facilitate in starting and growth of business not only for domestic firms but also for foreign firms. Against this background, Chapter 2 attempts to elaborate the various factors that encourage the growth of business in the region. In Chapter 2, the factors that hinder the expansion of business in the region are explored.

Chapter 3 — Impact of FDI on the Host and Home Country

Both inflow and outflow of FDI affect the host and source countries differently. Further, the impact can be positive or negative.

Chapter 3 makes an attempt to elaborate these impacts in both host and source countries.

Chapter 4 — Trends of Trade and Investment in the SAARC Region

In Chapter 4, the profile and trends in foreign direct investment and trade in the SAARC countries are presented. The chapter also discusses the evolution of FDI policy in the member countries of the SAARC region. The chapter is divided into five sections for each member country.

Chapter 5 — The Relationship between Trade and Investment in the SAARC Region

The surge in the volume of world trade and FDI in the last two decades has attracted a debate among the researchers and policymakers on the issue of the relationship between the two. The major question that arises is: how are they related? If related, is the relationship supplementary or complementary to each other, i.e. whether FDI enhances trade or contracts trade? These issues are addressed in Chapter 5.

Chapter 6 — Causal Relationship between Investment and Trade in the SAARC Region: An Analysis

One of the arguments for attracting FDI is that it encourages foreign trade. In Chapter 6, therefore, an attempt has been made to find the causal relationship between trade and investment. The analysis has been carried out for the entire region as a whole. The result of the analysis indicates that there is no causal relationship between trade and FDI among the SAARC countries.

Chapter 7 — A SUR Analysis of Investment and Institutional Variables

Apart from policy reforms, other institutional factors like business freedom, investment freedom, trade freedom, financial freedom, fiscal freedom, etc. of the host country may also affect foreign investment. The role of these factors has been addressed in Chapter 7 in the context of the SAARC region.

Chapter 8 — Summary and Conclusion

Finally, in the last chapter, summary and conclusion have been provided. The findings of the book are also presented in Chapter 8 along with their policy implications.

References

Adewumi, S. (2007). The Impact of FDI on Growth in Developing Countries: An African Experience (Dissertation).

Agrawal, P. (2000). Savings, Investment and Growth in South Asia, Indira Gandhi Institute of Development Research, 1–47.

Ahamed, M. G., & Tanin, F. (2010). Determinants of, and the Relationship between FDI and Economic Growth in Bangladesh, MPRA Paper 20236, University Library of Munich, Germany.

Alfaro, L. (2003). *Foreign Direct Investment and Growth: Does the Sector Matter?* Harvard Business School: Mimeo, Boston, MA.

Ali, F. A. A. (2010). Essays on Foreign Direct Investment, Institutions, and Economic Growth, Doctoral dissertation, University of Glasgow.

Athukorala, P. C., & Kishor, S. (2004). Foreign Investment in a Least Developed Country: The Nepalese experience, ASARC Working Papers, The Australian National University, Australia South Asia Research Centre.

Athukorala, P. P. A. W. (2003). The Impact of Foreign Direct Investment for Economic Growth: A Case Study in Sri Lanka. In *9th International Conference on Sri Lanka Studies*, Vol. 92, pp. 1–21.

Athukorala, P C. & Sharma, K. (2006). Foreign Investment in a Least Developed Country: the Nepalese Experience. *Transnational Corporations*, 15(2), 125.

Atique, Z., Ahmad, M. H., Azhar, U., & Khan, A. H. (2004). The Impact of FDI on Economic Growth under Foreign Trade Regimes: A Case Study of Pakistan, *The Pakistan Development Review*, 43(4), 707–718.

Balamurali, N., & Bogahawatte, C. (2004). Foreign Direct Investment and Economic Growth in Sri Lanka, *Sri Lankan Journal of Agricultural Economics*, 6(1), 37–50.

Balasubramanyam, V. N., Salisu, M., & Sapsford, D. (1996). Foreign Direct Investment and Growth: New Hypothesis and Evidence, *Economic Journal*, 106, 92–105.

Barrell, R., & Pain, N. (1996). An Econometric Analysis of US Foreign Direct Investment, *The Review of Economics and Statistics*, 200–207.

Beugelsdijk, S., Smeets, R., & Zwinkels, R. (2008). The Impact of Horizontal and Vertical FDI on Host's Country Economic Growth, *International Business Review*, 17(4), 452–472.

Bhagwati, J. N. (1978). *Anatomy and Consequences of Exchange Control Regimes*, Balinger Publishing: New York, NY.

Bista, R. B. (2010). Liberalization and Productivity Growth in Nepal: A Case of FDI Firm. In *18th International Input–Output Conference*, 20–25 June, Sydney.

Blomstrom, M., & Kokko, A. (1997). Regional Integration and Foreign Direct Investment, NBER Working Paper, No. 6019.

Blomstrom, M., Lipsey, R. E., & Zejan, M. (1994). What Explains Developing Country Growth? National Bureau of Economic Research, Working Paper no. 4132.

Borensztein, E., De Gregorio, J., & Lee, J.-W. (1998). How does Foreign Direct Investment Affect Economic Growth? *Journal of International Economics*, 45(1), 115–135.

Brown, R. L., Durbin, J., & Evans, J. M. (1975). Techniques for Testing the Constancy of Regression Relationships over Time. *Journal of the Royal Statistical Society.* Series B (Methodological), 149–192.

Caves, R. E. (1996). *Multinational Enterprise and Economic Analysis*, Cambridge University Press.

Chakraborty, C., & Nunnenkamp, P. (2008). Economic Reforms, FDI, and Economic Growth in India: A Sector Level Analysis, *World Development*, 36(7), 1192–1212.

Chen, C., Chang, L., & Zhang, Y. (1995). The role of foreign direct investment in China's post-1978 Economic Development. *World Development*, 23(4), 691–703.

Djurovic, A. B. (2011). FDI Impact on the Economic Growth in the Developing Countries (2000–2010), *Economic Development*, 2–3, 160–175.

Dutt, A. K. (1997). The Pattern of Direct Foreign Investment and Economic Growth, *World Development*, 25(11), 1925–1936.

Engle, R. F., & Granger, C. (1987). Co-intergration and Error-correction: Representation, Estimation and Testing, *Econometrica*, 49(4), 1057–1072.

Ethier, W. J. (1986). The Multinational Firm, *The Quarterly Journal of Economics*, 805–834.

Falki, N. (2009). Impact of Foreign Direct Investment on Economic Growth in Pakistan, *International Review of Business Research Papers*, 5(5), 110–120.

Farkas, B. (2012). Absorptive Capacities and the Impact of FDI on Economic Growth, Discussion Paper, DWI, Berlin.

Findlay, R. (1978). Relative Backwardness, Direct Foreign Investment, and the Transfer of Technology: A Simple Dynamic Model, *The Quarterly Journal of Economics*, 1–16.

Fry, M. J. (1993). *Foreign Direct Investment in a Macroeconomic Framework: Finance, Efficiency, Incentives and Distortions*, 1141, World Bank Publications.

Granger, C. W. (1969). Investigating Causal Relations by Econometric Models and Cross-Spectral Methods, *Econometrica: Journal of the Econometric Society*, 424–438.

Hansen, H., & Rand, J. (2006). On the Causal Links between FDI and Growth in Developing Countries, *The World Economy*, 29(1), 21–41.

Iftikhar, A. (2012). Foreign Direct Investment and Economic Growth in Selected SAARC Countries: A Causality Investigation Using Heterogeneous Panel Analysis. *Interdisciplinary Journal of Contemporary Research in Business*, 4(3).

Javed, K., Falak, S., Awan, R. U., & Ashfaq, M. (2012). Foreign Direct Investment, Trade, and Economic Growth: A Comparison of Selected South Asian Countries, *International Journal of Humanities and Social Science*, 2(5).

Johansen, S. (1991). Estimation and Hypothesis Testing of Co-integration Vectors in Gaussian Vector Autoregressive Models, *Econometrica: Journal of the Econometric Society*, 1551–1580.

Johnson, A. (2006). The Effects of FDI Inflows on Host Country Economic Growth, The Royal Institute of Technology, Centre of Excellence for Studies in Science and Innovation.

Jovanovic, N. M. (1998). *International Economic Integration*, Routledge: London.

Kindleberger, C. P. (1969). American Business Abroad, *The International Executive*, 11(2), 11–12.

Kumar, K. (1982). Third World Multinationals: A Growing Force in International Relations, *International Studies Quarterly*, 397–424.

Kumar, N. (2005). Liberalisation, Foreign Direct Investment Flows, and Development: Indian Experience in the 1990s, *Economic and Political Weekly*, 1459–1469.

Lall, S., & Streeten, P. (1977). *Foreign Investment, Transnationals, and Developing Countries*, Macmillan: London.

Mengistu, B., & Adams S. (2007). Foreign Direct Investment, Governance, and Economic Development in Developing Countries, *The Journal of Social, Political, and Economic Studies*, 32(2), 223–249.

OECD (2002). Foreign Direct Investment for Development: Maximizing Benefits, Minimizing Costs, OECD, Paris.

Pradhan, R. P. (2008). Does Economic Growth Promote Foreign Direct Investment? Evidence from Indiana and Malaysia, *South Asian Journal of Management*, 15(1), 7–23.

Quader, S. M. (2009). Foreign Direct Investment in Bangladesh: An Empirical Analysis on its Determinants and Impacts, *Asian Economic Review*, 52(1), 1–16.

Rayome, D., & Baker, J. C. (1995). Foreign Direct Investment: A Review and Analysis of the Literature, *The International Trade Journal*, 9(1), 3–37.

Sahoo, P. (2006). Foreign Direct Investment in South Asia: Policy, Trends, Impact, and Determinants, ADB Institute Discussion Paper no. 56.

Sarode, S. (2012). Effects of FDI on Capital Account and GDP: Empirical Evidence from India, *International Journal of Business and Management*, 7(8), 102.

Sengupta, N., & Banik, A. (1997). Regional Trade and Investment: Case of SAARC, *Economic and Political Weekly*, 2930–2931.

Singer, H. W. (1950). The Distribution of Gains between Investing and Borrowing Countries, *The American Economic Review*, 473–485.

Sodersten, B. (1970). International Economics, Harper and Row: New York, NY.

Tabassum, U., Nazeer, M., & Siddiqui, A. A. (2012). Impact of FDI on Import Demand and Export Supply Functions of Pakistan: An Econometric Approach, *Journal of Basic & Applied Sciences*, 8, 151–159.

UNCTAD (2007). World Investment Report, UNCTAD, Geneva.

Yousaf, M. M., Hussain, Z., & Ahmad, N. (2008). Economic Evaluation of Foreign Direct Investment in Pakistan, *Pakistan Economic and Social Review*, 37–56.

Yousaf, U., Nasir, A., Naqvi, F. N., Haider, A., & Bhutta, A. N. (2011). Impact of Foreign Direct Investment on Economic Growth of Pakistan, *European Journal of Economics, Finance and Administrative Sciences*, (32), 95–100.

Zellner, A. (1962). An Efficient Method of Estimating Seemingly Unrelated Regressions and Tests for Aggregation Bias, *Journal of the American Statistical Association*, 57(298), 348–368.

Chapter 2

Ease and Difficulty of Doing Business in South Asia

There are a number of factors that facilitate the starting and growth of domestic as well as foreign firms. These may be in the form of infrastructural development, easy documentation procedure, or a conducive regulatory regime. As against that, various factors also pose a threat to the flourishing of a business. All these factors exist almost in all the countries in different forms to different extents. South Asia also faces many of these issues. Being a developing region, South Asia faces many such difficulties, which deter the growth of business in the region to its potential. However, it also enjoys many facilities that make business easier. These factors are represented in the Ease of Doing Business Report of the World Bank. It is in this background the current chapter makes an attempt to elaborate on the various factors that simplify the growth of a business in the region. Along with the positive factors, the chapter also displays those factors that deter the growth of a business in the region.

2.1. Background

The performance of a business entity depends largely on the environment or the atmosphere that exists in the country. A positive environment with facilities and incentives help the existing businesses to grow while attracting others to invest. The business environment by and large consists of various indicators of the economy like banking and credit facilities, transportation facilities, labor market, and many more. Many attempts have been made to assess the performance of these indicators. Some of them captured the performance of individual indicators (e.g. logistic performance index, capital market index) while some tried to capture consolidated indicator's performance. One of the most popular and widely accepted indexes that assesses the performance of various indicators of the economy and presents them in a single indicator is the Ease of Doing the Business index. The ranking in the index reflects the existing business environment in a country and also indicates how easy it is to start a business in that country. This index is being prepared by the World Bank since 2003. The index consolidates performance of 10 different indicators ranging from getting electricity to getting credit. The index compares the performance of 190 countries around the world.

The Ease of Doing Business index measures aspects of business regulation and their implications for establishing a firm and its operations. It does not include all the issues that are relevant for making business decisions, but it does cover important areas that are under the control of policymakers. The Ease of Doing Business index focuses on key areas of interaction between the government and entrepreneurs, where policymakers and regulators can directly influence procedures to facilitate these interactions. The Ease of Doing Business index places emphasis on the quality of legal infrastructure and the strength of legal institutions. The protecting minority investors indicator set, for example, measures the protection of minority shareholders. The overall measure of the ease of doing business gives an indication of where it is easier for domestic small and medium-sized firms to do business. The ranking of economies on the basis of "ease of doing business" on a regular interval is a worthy practice as it helps to evaluate the best practices in governance. By formally putting down the states on a scale, benchmarking becomes easier and they can work toward improving their position. Although the economies with the most business-friendly regulations in this year's ease of doing business ranking are relatively diverse, the economies within the top 20 share some common features. The rankings are the assessment of the regulatory performance of the countries and a measure of how they improve over a period of time. The ranking depicts the performance of the economies in implementing a reform measure within a time frame.

The ease of doing business report covers all the eight countries in the South Asian region. The performance of these countries varies largely from each other. Variation exists both in the individual and aggregate levels. A descriptive analysis of the ranking of the individual South Asian countries is presented in the following sections.

2.1.1. *India*

With its population of more than 1.3 billion, growing middle class and rising disposable income of the citizens, India became a promising market to the investors across the world. It is evident from the ever-growing FDI in India in almost all the sectors of the economy. World Investment Report 2017 observed that India is the ninth highest recipient of FDI in the world and biggest in the South Asian region. Since the adoption of New Economic Policy in 1991, India has constantly strived to provide a conducive business environment to all its investors. A series of reform measures undertaken by the government has given a further boost to attracting foreign investment. The efforts made by the government is reflected in India's recent graduation in the ranking of Doing Business Report, 2018 prepared by the World Bank. The World Bank's Doing Business Report 2018 ranked India 100th out of the 190 countries surveyed. India has made remarkable progress in its ranking and jumped 30 places above from its earlier rank of 130 in the year 2017. India has shown the highest jump in rank among all countries this year.

India's performance continued in Doing Business Report, 2019, which placed India at the 77th position. This time India jumped 23 places compared to its ranking at the 100th position during 2018. India also ranked among the 10 highest improving countries during 2018–2019. This reflects India's achievement in implementing various regulatory measures to support the business environment in the country.

The NDA government in New Delhi, which took over in 2014, was hailed in the report for taking several measures to boost its ranking. Among 37 reform measures introduced recently in India, one of the major steps was recapitalizing the public sector banks with an infusion of $32 billion. This includes 1.35 trillion rupees through recapitalization bonds and 760 billion rupees via budgetary support. The easy credit will spur investment in critical infrastructural and power projects. Another significant step undertaken by the current government was the introduction of the Bankruptcy and Insolvency Act, 2017 which is expected to lower the volume of the non-performing assets (NPAs) of the financial services sector.

In a recent move, the Government of India has also simplified the process of business incorporation by introducing the SPICe form (INC-32). This form effectively combines the application for the Permanent Account Number (PAN) and the Tax Account Number (TAN) into a single submission. Implementation of Goods and Service Tax (GST) by removing a host of indirect taxes and reform in the labor laws has largely helped India to achieve this rank.

Table 2.1 reflects India's ranking in the Ease of Doing Business report in 2018 and 2019. The data clearly show that India has remarkably performed in almost all the indicators in 2019 compared to 2018. The World Bank noted that out of 10 parameters, India had improved on six parameters: Starting a Business, Construction Permits, Trading across Borders, Getting Electricity, Getting Credit, and Enforcing Contracts. The time for starting a business has been reduced from 30 days to 17 days, which improved its individual ranking from 156 in 2018 to 137 in 2019. The cost for completing all procedures to build a warehouse has been slashed to 5.4% of the warehouse value, from the earlier 23%. The total time needed for obtaining a permit has been reduced to 95 days, from 144 days. The ranking of the parameter "Construction Permit" improved remarkably from 181 in 2018 to 52 in 2019. The digitalization of trade facilities has helped reduce time to export documentation from 38 to only two hours while for imports it has reduced from 61 to three hours. Thus, all these improvements in the individual indicators helped India to make substantial progress in the overall ranking (Doing Business, 2019). India graduated in the

Table 2.1:   India's Performance in the Ease of Doing Business Index

Indicators	In South Asia		In the World	
	2019	2018	2019	2018
Doing business average	1	2	77	100
Starting a business	5	6	137	156
Dealing with construction permits	1	6	52	181
Getting electricity	1	1	24	29
Registering property	5	3	166	154
Getting credit	1	1	22	29
Protecting investors	1	1	7	4
Paying taxes	2	2	121	119
Trading across borders	2	4	80	146
Enforcing contracts	4	4	163	164
Resolving insolvency	4	4	108	103

Note: Ease of Doing Business report collects data up to the month of May of the preceding year. So, 2019 report displays the performance of 2018.
Source: Ease of Doing Business Report 2018 and 2019. The World Bank.

regional ranking as well. India's ranking elevated to the first position
from the second position during 2018 and fourth in 2017 among the
South Asian countries.

Even after such a spectacular performance in the ranking, India
still needs to overcome many of its shortcomings. India needs to
address the issue of a long time that it takes in issuing a construction
permit, registration of a business, and even getting an electricity connection. India needs to resolve many of the complications regarding
its GST regime. Dispute settlement is another area where India needs
immediate focus; however, it is one of the most challenging tasks to
bring reform in this area considering India's judiciary system.

2.1.2. *Bangladesh*

Bangladesh is a hub of garment manufacturers from across the world.
Hundreds of foreign companies have been manufacturing their gar-

ments in Bangladesh for a long time. Bangladesh is the world's largest exporter of readymade garments after China. Along with garment manufacturers, a number of MNCs dealing with various other goods and services are also operating in Bangladesh. The Bangladesh government is also trying to provide a quality environment for their growth. Many infrastructural facilities have also been developed in the recent times. It has to be noted that the situation for foreign investors is getting better and Bangladesh is becoming more investment-friendly than many another developing countries. Bangladesh's elevation from a least developed nation (LDC) to a developing country also reflects its effort. However, the efforts made have not been reflected in its ranking in the Doing Business ranking. Bangladesh is ranked 176th among 190 economies in 2019 which decreased from 177 in 2018. Bangladesh's ranking in the Doing Business Report is constantly deteriorating since 2008 from the position of 115. Although different indicators of ease of doing business in Bangladesh is improving, still it is not sufficient to make a significant difference.

The ranking of Bangladesh in different categories in 2019 has not changed much compared to 2018 (Table 2.2). The rankings of

Table 2.2:   Bangladesh's Performance in Doing Business Index

Indicators	In South Asia		In the World	
	2019	2018	2019	2018
Doing business average	6	6	176	177
Starting a business	6	4	138	131
Dealing with construction permits	4	3	138	130
Getting electricity	6	6	179	185
Registering property	6	6	183	185
Getting credit	6	6	161	159
Protecting investors	5	5	89	76
Paying taxes	4	4	151	152
Trading across borders	6	6	176	173
Enforcing contracts	6	6	189	189
Resolving insolvency	5	5	153	152

Source: Doing Business Report 2018 and 2019. The World Bank.

indicators like Registering Property, Trading across Borders, and Paying Tax have shown a marginal change. Many factors have deteriorated in 2019 compared to the 2018 ranking. The highest change has been witnessed in the case of protecting investors. Here the ranking has reduced by 13 points. Only one indicator, Getting Electricity, has shown fairly positive performance during this period. It is clear from the data that there is an urgent need to undertake various reform measure to upgrade the ranking. More attention needs to be paid to developing infrastructure in the country to facilitate investments.

Bangladesh needs to improve a lot in terms of both aggregate ranking and individual ranking in the region. During 2018, most of the indicators have shown worst performance in the region.

2.1.3. *Nepal*

Starting and operating a business in Nepal is quite an easy process. Nepal allows any foreign investor to invest in Nepal in all the sectors of the economy with the only exception of a very few negative listed sectors. Nepal allows 100% foreign investment in most sectors. All foreign investment in Nepal is regulated and administered by the Foreign Investment and Technology Act (FITTA), 1992 and Industrial Enterprise Act (IEA), 1992. The Department of Industries in the government of Nepal is the nodal agency for implementation and administration of the Foreign Investment and Technology Transfer Act in Nepal. The government of Nepal is offering complete tax exemption of income tax for the first 10 years and 50% in exemption income tax for the next 5 years to the licensed person or entity commencing commercial production, transmission, or distribution of hydroelectricity within March 2024.

Nepal's proactiveness is also reflected in its ranking in the Doing Business Report. Nepal ranks third in the South Asian region and 105 in the world. Nepal has made exporting and importing easier by implementing the ASYCUDA World, an electronic data interchange system.

Nepal has recently made progress in institutional reforms on several fronts. However, it may take some time to be reflected in the international rankings, including the Doing Business Report. Nepal strengthened access to credit by operationalizing existing law on secured transactions that implements a functional and secured transaction system, and establishing a centralized, notice-based, modern collateral registry in the topic of "getting credit." In terms of "protecting minority investors," Nepal has also strengthened minority investor protection by requiring greater corporate transparency.

The data in Table 2.3 suggest that the overall ranking of Nepal has deteriorated in the Doing Business Report 2019 compared to the report published in 2018. The performance of all the individual indicators has degraded in the 2019 ranking with the only exception being "Starting a Business."

In South Asia, Nepal's ranking has remained largely unchanged in case of the individual indicators. In the item "Resolving Insolvency," Nepal has retained the top position in the region. Nepal's overall ranking in the Doing Business Report 2019 has slipped to the fourth position from the third position in 2018.

Table 2.3:   Nepal's Performance in the Doing Business Index

Indicators	In South Asia 2019	In South Asia 2018	In the World 2019	In the World 2018
Doing business average	4	3	110	105
Starting a business	3	3	107	109
Dealing with construction permits	5	5	148	157
Getting electricity	4	4	137	133
Registering property	2	2	88	84
Getting credit	3	3	99	90
Protecting investors	4	4	72	62
Paying taxes	5	3	158	146
Trading across borders	3	2	82	76
Enforcing contracts	2	2	154	153
Resolving insolvency	2	1	83	76

Source: Doing Business Report 2018 and 2019. The World Bank.

2.1.4. *Pakistan*

Although Pakistan practices a free and open economy, various infra-structural bottlenecks have left the country far behind. Poor energy supply, unfavorable labor market policy, political instability, and security concern are some of the prominent issues facing Pakistan. Pakistan's legal system provides incomplete protection for the acquisition and disposition of property rights. Many public officials face allegations of bribery, extortion, cronyism, nepotism, and patronage. However, the government is continuously striving to bring reforms in the economy. Very recent initiatives like online property registration and automation in cross-border trade have helped Pakistani traders quite handsomely. The other reforms included enhanced remedies to address cases of prejudicial transactions between interested parties in India; rules to clarify ownership and control structures in Bhutan; greater corporate transparency in Nepal; and facilitating legal action against directors in case of prejudicial transactions with interested parties in Pakistan. Various other reforms related to construction permit and environmental approval at the provincial level are also underway.[1]

Pakistan's ranking in the Ease of Doing Business Report improved in 2019 compared to its rank in 2018. Pakistan was placed at the 147th position in the ranking of 2018, which shifted to the 136th position in the latest report of 2019. Among the South Asian countries, Pakistan was only above Bangladesh and Afghanistan. A detailed indicator-wise performance of Pakistan in the Ease of Doing Business Report of 2018 and 2019 is presented in Table 2.4.

The data in Table 2.4 displays a mixed performance of various indicators that the Ease of Doing Business Report covers. Indicators like starting a business, registering property, and trading across borders have shown better performance from their earlier ranking while others have deteriorated or remained unchanged in the ranking.

---

[1] World Bank advises credit access to improve business environment (January 23, 2018). Retrieved from https://www.thenews.com.pk/print/271658-wb-advises-credit-access-to-improve-business-environment. Accessed May 30, 2018.

Table 2.4: Pakistan's Performance in the Ease of Doing Business Index

	In South Asia		In the World	
Indicators	2019	2018	2019	2018
Doing business average	5	5	136	147
Starting a business	4	5	130	142
Dealing with construction permits	6	4	166	141
Getting electricity	5	5	167	167
Registering property	4	5	161	170
Getting credit	4	4	112	105
Protecting investors	2	2	26	20
Paying taxes	6	6	173	172
Trading across borders	5	5	142	171
Enforcing contracts	3	3	156	156
Resolving insolvency	1	2	53	82

Source: Ease of Doing Business Report 2018 and 2019. The World Bank.

Upgradation in starting business indictors was contributed by the replacement of the need to obtain a digital signature for company incorporation with a less costly personal identification number. Pakistan also increased minority investor protections by making it easier to sue directors in case of prejudicial transactions with interested parties in both Karachi and Lahore.

2.1.5. *Bhutan*

Bhutan offers one of the best environments for business across the world. For a long time, Bhutan is maintaining solid growth and macroeconomic stability, which is mainly contributed by hydropower construction and supportive fiscal and monetary policy. The low rate of inflation, a stable exchange rate and accumulating international reserves have further boosted the country's stability. Bhutan has a stable political and economic environment. It has made tremendous progress in reducing extreme poverty and promoting gender equality. Since long, the public sector has been the main driver of economic growth, but the government also recognizes the importance of private sector growth. Economic diversification is now a higher priority, particularly with demographic shifts bringing more young people into the labor market. The government has acted to ensure greater security for property rights. Constraints on private sector development include an inefficient regulatory framework, significant non-tariff barriers to trade, and a rudimentary investment code.

Although Bhutan is not very well advanced in infrastructural and industrial development, it is one of the high-performing economies in the Ease of Doing Business ranking. Bhutan is ranked in the 75th position in the Ease of Doing Business Report 2018. This was the top rank among the South Asian countries. But, in the latest report, Bhutan's position slipped to the 81st position while it lost its top position to India. However, it still retained its top position in the region among many of the individual indicators.

This achievement of Bhutan has come mainly as a result of undertaking reform plan during the last 10 years. Bhutan has successfully implemented reform measures, which has improved access to credit and enabled protection of minority investors, making it easier to start a business, register property, and also enhance contract enforcement. As a part of the effort to improve the ranking in the Ease of Doing Business Report, Bhutan issued an executive order in April 2014 forming a "Doing Business Steering Committee" chaired by the Prime Minister with all 10 ministers as members and the Joint Secretary in the Ministry of Economic Affairs (MoEA) as a member secretary. Each minister in this committee has been given the responsibility of overseeing reforms in improving one indicator each out of the 10 Ease of Doing Business Report indicators.[2] All these efforts have enabled Bhutan to reach the top position in the

---

[2] Tenzing Lamsang (May 7, 2014). Each minister has been given one indicator to push Bhutan to the top 100 position in the global "Doing Business Indicators." *The Bhutanese*. Accessed on June 1, 2018. Retrieved from https://thebhutanese.bt/each-minister-given-one-indicator-to-push-bhutan-to-the-top-100-position-in-the-global-doing-business-indicators/.

Table 2.5:   Bhutan's Performance in the Ease of Doing Business Index

Indicators	In South Asia		In the World	
	2019	2018	2019	2018
Doing business average	2	1	81	75
Starting a business	2	2	91	88
Dealing with construction permits	3	2	88	82
Getting electricity	2	2	73	56
Registering property	1	1	54	56
Getting credit	2	2	85	77
Protecting investors	6	6	125	124
Paying taxes	1	1	15	17
Trading across borders	1	1	28	26
Enforcing contracts	1	1	28	25
Resolving insolvency	6	6	168	168

Source: Ease of Doing Business Report 2018 and 2019. The World Bank.

Ease of Doing Business Report 2018 among the South Asian economies. A detailed, indicator-wise performance of Bhutan is represented in Table 2.5.

The data in Table 2.5 shows Bhutan's ranking dropped in the Ease of Doing Business Report 2019 as compared to its ranking in 2018. Individual indicators have also shown an appalling performance in this ranking.

2.1.6. *Sri Lanka*

A supporting and encouraging environment is very much important for a flourishing business. It determines whether there are strong incentives for individuals to identify market opportunities and create wealth, jobs, and economic growth. An enabling environment that makes it easy for individuals to start businesses, run them, sell them, and shut them if they are not successful is the one that fosters national economic growth. The government of Sri Lanka is committed to the reform agenda of improving competitiveness, governance, and public financial management. Sri Lankan economy is evolving from a primarily rural-based economy to an urbanized economy focused on the manufacturing and service sectors. With support from the World Bank, Sri Lanka is carrying out fiscal reforms, improving public financial management, enhancing public and private investment opportunities, addressing infrastructure constraints, and improving competitiveness.

Although the government is carrying out a number of reforms, it is still struggling with streamlining the process of starting a new business. A rigid legal framework adopted by Sri Lanka makes it difficult for entrepreneurs to reduce their labor force. The cost of firing a worker in Sri Lanka is one of the highest in the world.[3] The government practices an extensive mechanism of price controls. The subsidies provided by the government also distort many of the sectors in the economy. All these have resulted in a low ranking of Sri Lanka in the Ease of Doing Business report. A detailed representation of individual indicators of doing a business report for Sri Lanka is given in Table 2.6.

Table 2.6: Sri Lanka's Performance in the Ease of Doing Business Index

Indicators	In South Asia		In the World	
	2019	2018	2019	2018
Doing business average	3	4	100	111
Starting a business	1	1	83	77
Dealing with construction permits	2	1	65	76
Getting electricity	3	3	84	93
Registering property	3	4	140	157
Getting credit	5	5	124	122
Protecting investors	3	3	38	43
Paying taxes	3	5	141	158
Trading across borders	4	3	93	86
Enforcing contracts	5	5	164	165
Resolving insolvency	3	3	92	88

Source: Ease of Doing Business Report 2018 and 2019. The World Bank.

---

[3] Index of Economic Freedom 2018. The Heritage foundation. Accessed on November 7, 2018. Retrieved from https://www.heritage.org/index/country/srilanka.

The data show that Sri Lanka's ranking has gone up from 111 in 2018 to 100 in 2019. Other variables have shown mixed performance during this time period. Sri Lanka's position at the regional level has also upgraded by one point in the region.

2.2. Barriers and South Asian Integration

There exist a number of factors that create an obstacle to trade. These factors may be different in forms like a documentary, physical infrastructure, law and order, political, or any other. Our selected South Asian countries are also not free from these obstacles. These obstacles vary from country to country. However, there also exist some common obstacles like corruption and road connectivity that prevail in the entire region. The issues of infrastructural constraint, political instability, and sometimes strained diplomatic relationship become deterrents for the process to move forward in case of bilateral trade and investment in the region.

Analyzing various issues in individual countries, we find that workers in Bangladesh are entitled to elect collective bargaining agents (CBAs) to negotiate their demands with the management. A trade union may be formed if 30% of employees support it. All trade unions need to be registered. There are 47 labor laws covering matters such as wages, industrial disputes, and working conditions. Foreign nationals can be employed as long as their number does not exceed 15% of the total number of employees. All these conditions pose an obstacle in the smooth operation of the business in Bangladesh. Most of the time, the trade unions make unfair demands and organize a strike against the management by disrupting the operation of the factory.

Disruption of work by trade union is also very common in India. Evidence also suggests trade union members resorting to hooliganism in various parts of India. A senior manager at an Indian steel factory was burnt to death in the eastern state of Orissa by a group of factory workers. A similar incident also happened in plants in Noida and Manesar in the northern parts of India. Under the Constitution of India, labor is a subject in the "concurrent list," under which both the central and state governments are competent to enact legislation, with certain matters being reserved for the center. There are several important Labor Acts since 1952, which are highly protective of laborers.

The labor law is highly restrictive from an investor point of view in Nepal. By modern commercial standards, it impedes business flexibility in many instances. There are protective labor laws relating to retrenchment, wages, and promotion.

Many of the previous Sri Lankan governments subscribed to a socialist political mind-set for ensuring development in the country. As a result, the protection of the workers' interest has always been accorded a priority. Labor interest is protected by the Industrial Dispute Act (1950) and subsequent amendments in that provision. The present nationalist government in Sri Lanka is also unwilling to change the current scenario. As a result, the legal framework frequently influences the ease of doing business, wage level, promotion and retrenchment options. The WDI data reveal that the firing cost of an employee in terms of weeks of wages in Sri Lanka during 2003 was 156 weeks. However, the same in 2009 has further deteriorated to 217 weeks, signifying the difficulty level in laying off an employee.

Corruption is another prominent issue that hurts the business in South Asia. India has long struggled with endemic corruption and it's still a problem. In spite of having a national-level movement, there is little impact on corruption. Many of the government initiatives have also not borne fruit. India ranks as the 81st among the 180 countries covered in the annual corruption index, prepared by the Berlin-based institute Transparency International (TI). It mentioned India as one of the "worst offenders" in the Asia-Pacific region.

India requires a long list of paper works to be done at the time of investment. This takes a long time as well, and it delays registering and starting a business. Transport infrastructure also poses a threat to business in several instances in India. Due to lack of dedicated freight corridors, it makes unnecessary delay in transportation of goods.

Seasonality is one of the key challenges for the tourism sector in Bhutan. Tourists in Bhutan are classified into two categories: "cultural tourists" who make up 80% of the total and the remaining "trekking tourists," with a few who combine a trek with a cultural tour. In addition to this, the very nature of cultural tourism does not result in repeat visitations — close to 90% of tourists over the last 5 years were visiting Bhutan for the first time. The problems get aggravated as Bhutan, a landlocked country, faces accessibility and infrastructure bottlenecks. Bhutan can be entered by only two routes: by Air from Paro in the west through a single airline (Druk Air) with concomitant capacity problems, and by road connectivity through the border town of Phuentsholing in south-western Bhutan. As such, tourism in Bhutan is regionally concentrated in west-central parts of the country.

Nepal's biggest bottleneck is infrastructure and it demands a large investment. This includes railway, road, and telecommunication. Water supply and electricity generation are less than adequate and large foreign investment is needed in these areas. Higher education and health sector also are important areas that are seeking foreign investment and good management practices.

Regarding technology transfer and automation, various companies brought forth several important issues. Everest Bank, one of the major commercial banks in Nepal, feels that Internet-based banking solutions are effectively being implemented in the industry and absorption level is quite satisfactory. Surya Nepal, a subsidiary of ITC India, takes up the effort to train people to handle new machines. For the company, automation is helping them to address the labor problem to some extent. On the contrary, Nepal Distilleries has taken up a combined approach. Some plants are fully automated and some are semi-automated. Many companies feel that skilled labor shortage is inhibiting them to make fully automated plants.

In order to remove soft skill-related obstacles, companies are undertaking various efforts. In the case of management practices, Dabur Nepal Pvt. Ltd. introduced management information system and structured marketing and procurement tools in the company. Asian Paints also is conducting a large number of programs for the skill development of their workers. Both the companies as well as Berger highlight that professionalism is slowly improving in Nepal with the introduction of a good accounting system, scientific approach to have a vendor–client relationship, apart from using the latest tools for marketing and promotion.

Getting skilled workers in key managerial positions is increasingly becoming a serious challenge for foreign enterprises operating in Sri Lanka. The problems for MNC operations arise from the fact that the focus of the education system in Sri Lanka rests on primary education, resulting in poor substitutability between an average worker (e.g. in India) and his/her local counterpart. This leads to lower labor productivity, consequently slashing edges in doing international business.

Although guided by the Board of Investment (BOI) incentives, several foreign investors in Sri Lanka, in the manufacturing sector, namely, in chemicals and metal products have brought in latest technologies, which has significantly influenced the technological plane of the local market as well. Garment sector provides one example of technology transfer. The local value addition was earlier barely 30%, the statutory requirement. However, the level of value addition has now increased to around 65%. For example, earlier services of designers had to be imported. This is no longer the case and local players can provide the needful services.

Under the value-added tax (VAT) regime in Sri Lanka, the net return is taxable, which sometimes acts as a considerable barrier in light of other existing taxes. For instance, in the telecom sector, a 20% telecom levy is imposed, in addition to the Nation Building Tax (NBT) and Economic Service Charge (ESC) (2%), which in aggregate adds to the nuisance.

Among the various policy initiatives, one area that is deemed insufficient by many observers is competition policy. While greater liberalization in other domains has significantly improved the potential for foreign investors in the region, there remain numerous obstacles to both foreign and domestic investments, such as weak property rights and passive competition policy. The region's weak contract enforcement and intellectual property rights (IPRs), high tariff barriers for the import of key inputs, and an ever-increasing tax burden are discouraging foreign investors from making FDI in the region. Many cases are pending in different courts in all the countries of the region regarding competition issues.

Bureaucratic inertia exists and time taken for processing various regulatory approvals is very high. Uncertain legal protection civil courts take a very long time to settle industrial disputes. Also there is no separate court for the expeditious settlement of trade disputes and dishonored checks, which takes a long time and is still uncertain even being a criminal offense. Public sector inefficiencies increase the cost of services and utilities. On the other hand, private sector inefficiencies increase the cost of production as a whole. Inefficiency both in the public and private sectors give a negative impression to the foreign investors about the region.

Quality and availability of infrastructure facilities are the most critical factors determining the quantum of investment flows into any country. Much of these efforts have already translated into visible signs of improvement in a few sectors notably telecom and bandwidth availability. However, there is still a lot that remains to be done and our analysis finds that the perception about the overall state of the infrastructure facilities in South Asia among foreign investors is not very encouraging.

2.3. Conclusion

The chapter here does not intend to vilify the images of the countries in South Asia, but it focused on the prominent factors that can have a significant impact on any business *vis-à-vis* its location. These factors affect business in both negative and positive forms. Some facilitate the growth of the business while some hamper that growth. Covering 10 very vital factors, the World Bank prepares one of its flagship reports, Doing Business Report covering 190 countries, which is published annually. The report ranks a country in terms of ease of doing business in that country. The chapter analyzed this factor in the context of each of the South Asian countries.

Various factors that pose challenges to the growth of a business have also been described in this chapter. The analysis finds that, although each country has its own prospects and challenges, most of them face common challenges. Transportation, credit facility, and corruption are found to be some common challenges faced by the region to various degrees.

Chapter 3

Impact of FDI on the Host and Home Country

Both inflows and outflows of FDI impact the host and source countries differently. The impact can be positive and negative. This chapter makes an attempt to explain these impacts in both host and source countries.

3.1. Defining FDI

Foreign direct investment (FDI) flows record the value of cross-border transactions related to direct investment during a given period of time, usually a quarter or a year. Financial flows consist of equity transactions, reinvestment of earnings, and intercompany debt transactions. FDI has been defined by various national and international bodies. The Benchmark Definition, Organisation for Economic Co-operation and Development (OECD, 2008, Fourth Edition) defines FDI as the category of international investment that reflects the objective of a resident entity in one economy to obtain a lasting interest in an enterprise resident in another economy. The lasting interest implies the existence of a long-term relationship between the direct investor and the direct investment enterprise and a significant degree of influence on the management of the enterprise. The direct or indirect ownership of 10% or more of the voting power of an enterprise resident in one economy by an investor resident in another economy is evidence of such a relationship.

The United Nations Conference on Trade and Development (UNCTAD) defines FDI as an investment involving a long-term relationship and reflecting a lasting interest and control by a resident entity in one economy in an enterprise resident in an economy other than that of the foreign direct investor. FDI implies that the investor exerts a significant degree of influence on the management of the enterprise operating in the other economy.

Various factors play an important role in attracting foreign investment and also an investor to invest outside the domestic market. Many economists have explained the reasons behind the international movement of capital and firms or investors making a direct investment in a foreign market. According to Hymer, technological superiority is the most important advantage for the foreign firm against the domestic firm and it facilitates the introduction of new products with new features. The technological advancement of the firm instigates it to invest in a foreign market (Hymer, 1976).

Sodersten (1970) also argued that willingness to increase profits by taking advantage of technological superiority or superior organizational structure was the main reason for direct investment by a foreign firm. Graham and Krugman (1989) stated that in the past it was the technological advantage possessed by European firms that had led to them investing in the United States.

Dunning (1993) suggested that a firm would engage in FDI if three conditions were fulfilled: (i) It should have ownership advantages *vis-à-vis* other firms (O); (ii) It is beneficial to internalize these advantages rather than to use the market to transfer them to foreign firms (I); and (iii) There are some location advantages in using a firm's ownership advantages in a foreign locale (L).

FDI is also made to take advantage of the low cost of production in the foreign market compared to the domestic market. Diversifying risk and developing or establishing as an international brand are also some of the vital motives for FDI. Thus, there exist various reasons for undertaking a foreign investment.

3.2. How FDI Impacts an Economy

FDI impacts both the host and source countries. The host countries that are poor or developing generally face a capital crunch for undertaking many of their economic activities. In this case, foreign capital investment can facilitate technology transfer and business know-how to developing economies. FDI may enhance the productivity growth of all firms not only those receiving the foreign capital but it also implies that the transfer of technology through FDI will have substantial spillover effects for the entire economy (Aurangzeb & Thanasis, 2014). During the last few decades, the significance of FDI has increased many fold. Countries have substantially been benefitted with the inflow of foreign capital. The much-needed capital for infrastructural development has not been fulfilled by FDI. Developing countries have started to see FDI as a source of economic development and modernization, income growth, and employment. Along with capital, FDI inflow also brings in advanced technical knowledge, modern supply chain management tools, and efficient managerial skills to the developing host countries. However, the impact of FDI is not limited to positive factors. It also carries a number of negative influences on the hosting economy such as overexploitation of the natural resources, exploiting workforce, competitive pressure on the domestic industry, and many more. An elaboration of these factors is done in Section 3.2.1.

3.2.1. *Impact of FDI inflows on the host country*

3.2.1.1. *Capital infusion*

The first and foremost impact that FDI makes on a host country is pumping of capital into the economy. FDI brings capital that is used for establishing business ventures. It means transfer of funds to purchase and acquire physical capital, such as factories and machinery. Frindlay (1978) argued that FDI is a way to improve a country's economic performance through the transmission effect of more advanced technologies introduced by multinationals. It increases the foreign capital reserve of the country and improves the balance of payment situation. Capital inflows can help finance a current account deficit. Both theory and empirical studies support the argument that FDI benefits the economic growth of developing countries. Urata (2002) argued that FDI has immensely befitted the economies of East Asian countries in their rapid economic growth during the late 1980s.

3.2.1.2. *Job creation*

One of the major concerns of the policymakers today is to create sufficient jobs for their workforce. The emergence of modern technologies like robotics and artificial intelligence, which displaces human labor, creates further concern for countries with high population. Unemployment is not a new phenomenon limited just to developing countries. Today, almost all the economies in the world are experiencing some degree of unemployment. Employment is another area that is affected by FDI inflows. A large number of jobs are created in the recipient country. When a manufacturing unit is set up in a country by a multinational corporation, it requires a huge labor force with different skill sets. Countries like India with a large number of both skilled and unskilled workers are immensely benefitted. The business process outsourcing (BPO) industry and software industry in India and the manufacturing sector of Taiwan are some of the examples in this regard. These industries have developed and are sustained almost entirely by foreign firms. Foreign companies help to increase the wage rate in a country. Most of the multinationals pay higher wages compared to domestic firms. This forces the domestic firms to increase their wages so as to hire competent labor with quality skills. Thus, the overall wage rate increases in the market.

Further, foreign companies provide skill training to the domestic labor force, making them aware of sophisticated technology and in the operation of new-age machinery. Empirical evidence suggests that considerable national and sectoral discrepancies persist. MNCs tend to provide more training and upgrading of human capital than do domestic enterprises. Human capital upgradation and spillovers are closely interrelated with technology diffusion. In particular, technologically advanced sectors and host countries are more likely to see human capital spillovers and, conversely, economies with a high human capital component lend themselves more easily to technology spillovers. Thus, FDI helps in fostering economic growth in the host country by increasing its productive capacity by improving the labor force.

3.2.1.3. *Technology diffusion*

Along with the capital, FDI brings modern technological know-how to the host economy. Economic literature recognizes technology diffusion as one of the most prominent channels through which the presence of foreign companies may bring positive externalities in the host developing economy. MNCs from the developed countries are the most important source of corporate research and development (R&D) activities, and they generally possess a higher level of technology that is available in developing countries, so they have the potential to generate considerable technological spillovers. However, whether and to what extent MNEs facilitate such spillovers varies according to context and sectors (OECD, 2002).

Economic literature describes that technology transfer and diffusion take place via four interrelated channels: (1) vertical linkages with suppliers or purchasers in the host countries; (2) horizontal linkages with competing or complementary companies in the same industry; (3) migration of skilled labor; and (4) the internationalization of R&D. It is also argued that the positive spillovers is strongest and most consistent in the case of vertical linkages, in particular, the "backward" linkages with the local suppliers in developing countries. MNCs generally are offering technical assistance, training and other information to raise the quality of the suppliers' products. Many MNCs also provide assistance to the local suppliers in purchasing raw materials and intermediate goods and in upgrading and standardizing production facilities.

3.2.1.4. *Expanding trade*

Although there exist different views on how FDI enhances trade or benefits trade of the host economy, there is an emerging school of thought that supports this view. The main trade-related benefit of FDI for developing countries lies in its long-term contribution to integrating the host economy more closely into the world economy in a process likely to include higher imports as well as exports. In other words, trade and investment are increasingly recognized as mutually reinforcing channels for cross-border activities.

Haddad and Harrison (1993) argued that FDI inflows help in expanding exports of domestic sectors through industrial linkage or spillover effects. This effect creates a strong demand for domestic products and promotes exports. FDI also augments export-oriented productivity, which further advances export performance. Export also contributes to overall economic growth by facilitating labor mobilization and capital accumulation.

In developing resource crunch economies, FDI plays a vital source of external finance, which closes the ever-increasing export–import imbalance. High export performance acts as a channel for fulfilling the much-needed foreign currency required to supplement inadequate domestic capital formation, a serious problem facing developing countries. Export-oriented FDI inflows can also be used to expand productive capacity, lower production costs, and obtain economies of scale.

3.2.1.5. *Bringing competition*

FDI, along with all the above-discussed factors, also brings competition in the domestic sector of the economy. The entry of multinational firms expands the supply of goods in the host country's market. Local manufacturers, in order to maintain their market shares, respond to this competition, leading to an increase in productivity and reduce prices. OECD (2002) points out that FDI has the potential to increase competitive pressures in the host country and that this rise is increased as the market is closed. These effects are directly related to the existing competition in the market and the response capacity of local firms.

Foreign firms often choose to form a joint venture with the local firms with competitive skills. Venturing into such an arrangement exposed the domestic firms to explore new territories. They are exposed to new managerial and supply chain facilities. Adopting and learning this modern and advanced know-how makes the domestic firms more commutative. This further induces other domestic firms to adopt upgraded technology. Thus, along with technology, FDI brings a competitive atmosphere in the economy. However, with the positive externalities, FDI may also bring negative and unhealthy competition for the domestic economy. Many of the firms that are not in the position to upgrade their technology and hire skilled human resource may be left behind in the competition, leading to the shutdown of their business. Many of the times, due to the high risk-taking capacity of the foreign firms and deep pockets to offer discounts and bear losses, domestic firms are driven out of the competition and eventually shut down their business.

3.2.2. *OFDI and its impact on the source economy*

Outward flows represent transactions where investors in the reporting economy increase their investment in enterprises in a foreign economy, such as through purchases of equity or reinvestment of earnings, less any transactions that decrease the investment in the reporting economy by investors in enterprises in a foreign economy, such as sales of equity or borrowing by the resident investor from the foreign enterprise.[1] In simple words, an investment made by an investor in a country in any other foreign country where the investing firm acquires voting right in the investee firm and satisfies the norms to be called as direct investment is referred as outward foreign direct investment[2] (OFDI hereafter).

Like inward FDI, OFDI also impacts the domestic or home country in various ways. Different indicators of the economy are impacted differently. The economic impact of outward FDI on the home country economy is perhaps the most controversial and one of the

---

[1] OECD (2017), FDI flows (indicator). doi: 10.1787/99f6e393-en (Accessed on 21 June 2017)
[2] See, Rao and Dhar (2011) for detail definition of Direct Investment.

frequently discussed topics in the outward FDI literature. Major concerns that have emerged during the last few years are that outward FDI shifts jobs and investments abroad and reduces employment and investing capacity of the investing firm in the domestic economy. OFDI is also criticized for containing export from the home country. Several scholars have raised their concern that the relocation of production activities could harm and reduce demand for domestic labor, which in turn could result in lower wages and higher unemployment, especially when the production is relocated to low-wage countries (Lipsey, 2004). The very recent decision of the US government to curb outsourcing and create domestic employment opportunities empirically justifies the concern.

3.2.2.1. *Impact on export from source economy*

Outward FDI may impact the home country in two ways. First, the investing firm may substitute exports from the home economy by relocating the production unit abroad. This will contain export volume from the home economy. Second, outward FDI may complement export of the home economy if it generates export demand for other products, such as intermediate goods or services that are in abundant in supply in the home economy. Instead of exporting finished goods to consumers in the host markets, parent firms of MNCs ship intermediate goods to their subsidiaries located in major export markets (Blomstrom & Kokko, 1994). Moreover, outward FDI could increase supplier exports to the host economy if the investment increases MNCs' sales and its demand for intermediate goods.

Various empirical studies have been conducted to assess the impact of OFDI on the export of the home economy. The available literature suggests a mixed result in this regard. Ellingsen, Likumahuwa and Nunnenkamp (2006) applied the gravity model to investigate the relationship between Singapore's outward FDI and trade for the manufacturing industries. The result finds that Singapore's FDI has not replaced exports. Similar results have also been demonstrated by Lipsey, Ramstetter and Blomström (2000) in the case of Japan and Svensson (1996) for Sweden.

As against the above studies, Lee, Lin and Tsui (2009) found a negative relationship between outward FDI and exports from the home county. The results suggest that outward FDI from the Asian countries to China negatively affects their exports to GDP ratio.

It is clear from the above discussion that OFDI may have both negative and positive impacts on the home country exports. However, here we feel that it is the nature of the FDI that can have a negative or positive impact. If the investment is made by a firm to cater to the foreign market, which it was serving through export earlier, it will definitely reduce the export. In other words, if the FDI is horizontal in nature, it will decrease the export volume of the home country proportional to the units it was exporting earlier. However, if the firm imports intermediary goods used to produce the final good from the home country, it will increase the export of the intermediate goods. In nutshell, it can be said that the impact of the OFDI depends on the complementary or supplementary nature of the investment.

3.2.2.2. *Impact on domestic investment in the home economy*

From a theoretical perspective, the impact of OFDI on the domestic investment of home country possibly will occur through financial markets and product markets (Herzer, 2010; Stevens & Lipsey, 1992). Through financial markets, outward FDI may discourage domestic capital accumulation if the capital transferred abroad (which is part of the domestic savings) increases interest rates in the home economy and makes borrowing more expensive for other domestic firms. This is, however, less likely if the country is open to international financial markets. The positive stimulus may come from the product market. Domestic investment may be stimulated if outward FDI increases market access for suppliers (Herzer, 2010). However, if FDI outflows complement the home country's exports through backward and forward production linkages, then such outflows may be seen as complementary to domestic investment. Therefore, FDI outflows may have positive, negative, or neutral effects on the home country's domestic investment rate.

A comprehensive list of empirical works is also available in the economic literature, which deals with the assessment of the impact of OFDI on domestic investment. An analysis done by Al-Sadig (2013) finds that that OFDI flows negatively impact domestic investment. Another work by Jaklic and Svetlicic (2003) could not find that outward FDI of Slovenian MNCs dampens investment in the Slovenian home economy. By contrast, home country investment is stimulated significantly by activities abroad. Similar findings are presented by Wu, Mun and Ho (2003) in the case of Singapore. They find that Singaporean foreign investments have a statistically significant long-run impact on the domestic investment.

3.2.2.3. *Impact on employment in the home economy*

The impact of outward FDI on domestic employment is usually related to the nature of that FDI, namely, whether it is vertical or horizontal. Accordingly, it has been claimed in the literature that a substitution effect between employment in a foreign subsidiary and in the parent company occurs when the MNE operates in countries with similar factor endowments (i.e., the case of horizontal FDI). Conversely, when the MNE invests in a low-cost host country (i.e., the case of vertical FDI), its competitiveness could increase by taking advantage of scale economies, which may lead to an increase in home country employment. In other terms, the scale effect would dominate over the substitution effect for the parent firm, so employment in the home country might increase. On the other hand, this classification of FDI is similar to the distinction among resource-seeking, market-seeking, and efficiency-seeking investments. Specifically, resource-seeking investments would be aimed at acquiring some particular resources abroad, both natural and human, of a better quality or at a lower cost than in the home country of the firm, whereas the aim of market-seeking investments would be entering a market that is new for the firm. Finally, efficiency-seeking investments would be those looking for relatively cheaper labor. The net effect on employment of these different types of FDI is not clear cut, however (Agarwal, 1997).

Another aspect that has drawn the attention of researchers is the possible impact of outward FDI on the domestic demand for skilled and unskilled labor. In particular, unskilled workers might lose when the MNEs move part of the value chain to low-wage countries in order to save labor costs (i.e., the case of vertical FDI), whereas skilled workers are likely to lose when MNEs move some skill-intensive tasks abroad (i.e., the case of horizontal FDI). In a research work, using data for Japanese MNEs over the period 1965–1990, Head and Ries (2002) found that FDI in low-income countries appeared to raise skill intensity at home, with such effect falling as FDI shifted toward high-income countries. Similar results were obtained by Hansson (2005), for the case of Swedish MNEs in the 1990s, and by Cuyvers, Dhyne and Soeng (2010), who analyzed FDI by Belgian firms in the period 1997–2007. On the other hand, Driffield, Love and Taylor (2009) found a negative impact of outward FDI on both skilled and unskilled labor demand in the UK over the period 1987–1996; the impact went stronger over time, and especially for unskilled workers, since investment into low-cost locations predominated within UK's outward FDI. In the same line, Elia, Mariotti and Piscitello (2009) showed that foreign involvement by Italian firms over the years 1996–2002 had a negative impact upon the demand for low-skilled workers in the parent company's "industrial region" but also on the demand for high-skilled workers when FDI outflows were addressed to high-income countries.

3.3. Concluding Remarks

The chapter described the possible impacts of FDI inflows and outflows on the host and source country of the investment. The chapter also covered various variables of the economy, namely, employment, export, and investment which are highly impacted by the inward as well as outward FDI. In the case of inflows, these factors impact the host economy while outflow impacts the source economy. The chapter also discussed the theoretical viewpoint of the FDI as well as the empirical works that were conducted in this regard. Some studies have found the positive impact of FDI while some have established a negative impact of FDI. However, there is no consensual result of the same. It can be concluded saying that the impacts of FDI on the home country of the investing firm depend on the nature and motives of the investing firm. And for the host country, it depends on its readiness and the capacity to absorb the knowledge and competitive strength to stand against the foreign firms.

References

Agarwal, J. P. (1997). Effect of Foreign Direct Investment on Employment in Home Countries, *Transnational Corporations*, 6, 1–28.

Al-Sadig, A. J. (2013). Outward Foreign Direct Investment and Domestic Investment: The Case of Developing Countries, IMF Working Paper, 13/52.

Aurangzeb, Z., & Thanasis, S. (2014). The Role of Foreign Direct Investment (FDI) in a Dualistic Growth Framework: A Smooth Coefficient Semi-Parametric Approach, *Borsa Istanbul Review*, 14(3), 133–144.

Blomström, M., & Kokko, A., (1994). Home-Country Effects of Foreign Direct Investment: Sweden. In Globerman, S. (ed.), *Canadian-Based Multinationals*, University Calgary Press: Calgary, Alberta, Canada, 341–364.

Cuyvers, L., Dhyne, E., & Soeng, R. (2010). The Effects of Internationalization on Domestic Labour Demand by Skills: Firm-level Evidence for Belgium, Working Paper 206, National Bank of Belgium.

Driffield, N., Love, J. H., & Taylor, K. (2009). Productivity and Labour Demand Effects of Inward and Outward Foreign Direct Investment on UK Industry, *The Manchester School*, 77, 171–203.

Dunning, J. H. (1993). *The Globalization of Business*, Routledge: London.

Elia, S., Mariotti, I., & Piscitello, L. (2009). The Impact of Outward FDI on the Home Country's Labour Demand and Skill Composition, *International Business Review*, 18, 357–372.

Ellingsen, G., Likumahuwa, W., & Nunnenkamp, P. (2006). Outward FDI by Singapore: A Different Animal? *Transnational Corporations*, 15(2), 1–40.

Frindlay, R. (1978). Relative Backwardness, Direct Foreign Investment, and the Transfer of Technology: A Simple Dynamic Model, *Quarterly Journal of Economics*, 92, 1–16.

Graham, E. M., & Krugman, P. (1989). Foreign Direct Investment in USA, Institute for International Economics, Washington D.C.

Haddad, M., & Harrison, A. (1993). Are There Positive Spillovers from Direct Foreign Investment? Evidence from Panel Data for Morocco, *Journal of Development Economics*, 42, 51e74.

Hansson, P. (2005). Skill Upgrading and Production Transfer within Swedish Multinationals, *Scandinavian Journal of Economics*, 107, 673–692.

Head, K., & Ries, J. (2002). Offshore Production and Skill Upgrading by Japanese Manufacturing Firms, *Journal of International Economics*, 58, 81–105.

Herzer, D. (2010). Outward FDI and Economic Growth, *Journal of Economic Studies*, 37(5), 476–494.

Hymer, S. H. (1976). *The International Operation of National Firms: A Study of Direct Foreign Investment*, MIT Press: Cambridge, MA.

Jaklic, A., & Svetlicic, M., (2003). *Enhanced Transition Through Outward Internationalization: Outward FDI by Slovenian Firms*, Ashgate Publishing: Farnham, UK.

Lee, H. Y., Lin, K. S., & Tsui, H. C. (2009). Home Country Effects of Foreign Direct Investment: From a Small Economy to a Large Economy, *Economic Modelling*, 26(5), 1121–1128.

Lipsey, R. E. (2004). Home-and host-country effects of foreign direct investment. In *Challenges to globalization: Analyzing the economics* (pp. 333–382). University of Chicago Press.

Lipsey, R. E., Ramstetter, E., & Blomström, M. (2000). Outward FDI and Home Country Exports: Japan, the United States, and Sweden, SSE/EFI Working Paper Series in Economics and Finance, 369.

OECD (2002). *Foreign Direct Investment for Development: Maximising Benefits, Minimising Costs*, OECD: Paris.

OECD (2008). *Benchmark Definition of Foreign Direct Investment*, Fourth Edition, OECD: Paris.

Rao, K. S. C., & Dhar, B. (2011), India's FDI Inflows: Trends and Concepts, Working Paper No. 138, IIID, New Delhi.

Sodersten, B. (1970). *International Economics*, Harper and Row: New York, NY.

Stevens, G. V. G., & Lipsey, R. E. (1992). Interactions between Domestic and Foreign Investment, *Journal of International Money and Finance*, 11(1), 40–62.

Svensson, R. (1996). Effects of Overseas Production on Home Country Exports: Evidence Based on Swedish Multinationals, *Weltwirtschaftliches Archiv*, 132(2), 304–329.

Urata, S. (2002). Japanese Foreign Direct Investment in East Asia with Particular Focus on ASEAN4. In *Conference on Foreign Direct Investment: Opportunities and Challenges for Cambodia, Laos, and Vietnam*, Hanoi, Vietnam, 16–17 August.

Wu, F., Mun, H. T., & Ho, T., (2003). Outward Foreign Direct Investment and Its Impact on the Home Economy: The Case of Singapore, *Journal of Asian Business*, 19(3), 27–48.

Chapter 4

Trends of Trade and Investment in SAARC Countries

The current chapter displays the trends of trade and investment flows in the SAARC nations. Country-wise analysis of the trends in trade and investment has been carried out. The analysis includes the major trading goods, sources, and destination of trade. The chapter also discloses the major sectors where FDI flows have occurred.

4.1. Introduction

This chapter analyzes the profile of investment flows in the SAARC countries. The chapter is organized as follows. Each section is devoted to a particular SAARC country. Due to the paucity of comparable and relevant data, three member countries, namely, Pakistan, Afghanistan, and Maldives, could not be analyzed. Further, for the selected countries, the same pattern or format could not be followed in the analysis due to paucity in data. The time period selected for individual countries was also influenced by the availability of data.

It is evident from the available data that South Asian countries, especially India, have become the most attractive destinations for FDI inflows in the recent past. UNCTAD (2017) ranks India ninth in the global FDI destinations, followed by Pakistan and Sri Lanka in terms of attracting FDI in the region. India accounts for around

90% of the FDI flows in the region. FDI as a share of GDP also varies largely in this group of countries. The differences also reflect in the geographical size, stages of development, availability of basic infrastructure, the regulatory frameworks on FDI, and the size of the economies themselves among others. However, with all the available pros and cons, all the economies have performed fairly well in attracting FDI, especially in the last two decades. The investment in the region has come from various quarters of the world and has moved to various sectors of the economy. In this context, the following sections depict the country-wise trend of FDI flows in the region.

4.2. Bangladesh

4.2.1. *Background*

The economy of Bangladesh experienced a rapid growth in the past few years. The World Bank data reveal that Bangladesh's GDP growth rate during 2016 was 7.1%. Its per capita income in 2016 was $3579 (adjusted by purchasing power parity). According to the International Monetary Fund (IMF), Bangladesh ranked as the 44th largest economy (nominal terms) in the world in 2016, with a gross domestic product of $221.4 billion. More than half the GDP comes from the service sector; the majority of Bangladeshi population is employed in the agriculture sector, while ready-made garments (RMGs), textiles, leather, jute, fish, vegetables, leather and leather goods, and ceramics are important industrial produce. The real GDP grew by 7.3% in 2016–2017, and was 5.7% in 2010–2011.[1] The agriculture sector grew at 3% in 2016–2017 as against 4.1% in 2010–2011. Industrial sector growth was 10% in 2016–2017, an increase from 6.5% in 2010–2011. The service sector was the highest contributor to the economy and in growth terms achieved 6.7% in 2016–2017 as compared to 6.3% in 2010–2011.

---

[1] Annual Report, Bangladesh Bank, 2009–2010.

4.2.2. *FDI policy in Bangladesh*

In the late 1980s and the 1990s, Bangladesh announced a liberalized FDI policy framework. In recent years, Bangladesh has extensively improved its investment and regulatory environment, including the liberalization of the industrial policy, the abolition of performance requirements, and allowance of full foreign-owned joint ventures. In order to encourage the flow of FDI, EPZs were established. The capital markets were allowed to receive foreign portfolio investments in both primary and secondary markets. FDI is encouraged in almost all industrial activities excluding only the reserved sectors like the production of arms and ammunition, forest plantation, nuclear energy, and printing of currency. The foreign investment in Bangladesh is governed by the Foreign Private Investment Act 1980. This act adopts a non-discriminatory approach between foreign investment and local investment. The adoption of convertibility of currency in 1994 eased the way for investors by relaxing the rules regarding them from obtaining prior approval from the Bangladesh Bank for current account transactions.

Thus, the general investment law in Bangladesh is open to FDI. However, the scope and coverage are too limited, and this leaves plenty of room to regulate the FDI entry policy at the sector level. For example, there is a list of "controlled industries" in which ownership restrictions may apply and approval of the relevant ministry is required. Another example is high-growth industries, such as RMGs and pharmaceuticals, in which FDI is discouraged. An analysis of the Intellectual Property Rights (IPRs) suggests the adoption of a modern investment policy, along with other regulatory reforms, to address issues affecting the wider business environment.

The Foreign Private Investment Act 1980 has also been enacted to provide legal protection to foreign investors against nationalization and expropriation. The act guarantees repatriation of profit, capital, and dividend, and equitable treatment with local investors. IPRs, such as patents, designs and trademarks, and copyrights, are protected. Bilateral Investment Guarantee Agreements have also been signed with a number of countries. Bangladesh is a signatory to the multilateral bodies like The Multilateral Investment Guarantee (MIGA) and International Convention for Settlement of Investment Dispute (ICSID) and is also a member of World Intellectual Property Organization (WIPO) and the World Association of Investment Promotion Agencies (WAIPA). The FDI policy of Bangladesh allows free repatriation of profits, and the Bangladeshi currency Taka (Tk) is almost fully convertible on the current account. Bangladeshi policy does not require prior approval for FDI inflows. However, a foreign investor needs to register itself with the Board of Investment (BOI).

4.2.3. *Trends in FDI inflows*

At the time of independence in 1971, Bangladesh inherited only a small stock of FDI, most of it by TNCs and geared toward exploiting a domestic market protected by the then prevailing import-substitution policy. Since then, Bangladesh has been trying hard to attract foreign investment and has also been successful to a large extent. The effort made by Bangladeshi authorities is reflected in the data presented in Figure 4.1. Data of FDI inflows reveal a fluctuating trend. In the year 2000, the inflows of FDI were little higher than the US $500 million, but this increased to more than $2000 million in 2015.

Tables 4.1 and 4.2 give an indication of the sector-wise investments made in the region for both FDI (100%) and joint ventures. The tables show that largest investments were made in the agriculture,

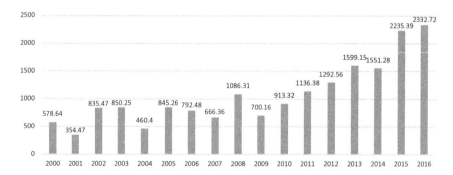

Figure 4.1:   Year-wise Inflow of Actual Investment to Bangladesh (Million USD)

Source: Authors' calculation based on BOI data, Bangladesh.

Table 4.1:   Sector-wise Investments in Bangladesh (100% FDI)

S. No.	Sectors	No. of Units	Investment (Million USD)	Employment Opportunities (Person)
1.	Agro-based	59	154.29	24,434
2.	Chemical	65	1985.93	6147
3.	Engineering	57	38.96	4388
4.	Food and Allied	13	19.11	1662
5.	Glass and Ceramics	3	8.188	328
6.	Printing Publishing and Packaging	7	2.26	325
7.	Tannery and Rubber Products	4	4.013	602
8.	Textile	115	221.25	84,578
9.	Services	91	4575.90	18,758
10.	Miscellaneous	7	2.834	735
	Total	**418**	**7012.76**	**141,957**

Note: 100% foreign investments came to Bangladesh in the sectors indicated (1990–2010).
Source: Investment Implementation Monitoring Cell (IIMC), Board of Investment, Bangladesh, 2010.

Table 4.2:   Sector-wise Investments in Bangladesh (Joint Ventures)

S. No.	Sectors	No. of Units	Investment (Million USD)	Employment Opportunities (Person)
1.	Agro-based	111	329.80	24,434
2.	Chemical	169	1413.02	21,319
3.	Engineering	151	412.82	18,847
4.	Food and Allied	50	54.65	3,069
5.	Glass and Ceramics	15	69.42	2,334
6.	Printing Publishing and Packaging	13	17.15	877
7.	Tannery and Rubber Products	42	85.75	17,219
8.	Textile	320	1093.16	135,053
9.	Services	301	6693.35	47,394
10.	Miscellaneous	8	3.31	507
	Total	**1179**	**10,172.47**	**259,207**

Note: The joint venture investment registered with BOI (1990–2010) are indicated.
Source: Investment Implementation Monitoring Cell (IIMC), Board of Investment, Bangladesh, 2010.

chemical, engineering, and food, and allied sectors. However, the current crisis in the power sector requires investments to uplift itself. The data in Table 4.1 reveal that the service sector has attracted the highest amount of investment for Bangladesh from 1990 to 2010. The service sector is followed by the chemical sector, which attracted more than $1985 million. However, the highest employment was created by the textile sector.

The data provided in Table 4.2 shows that a total of 1179 joint ventures were established in various sectors of the Bangladesh economy during 1990–2010. These joint venture firms attracted $10 billion of FDI. It also provided employment opportunities to more than 259,207 persons during our reference period. The highest number of the joint ventures were established in the textile sector, followed by the service sector. These joint venture firms created 135,053 jobs for Bangladeshi people.

The inward FDI in Bangladesh during 2015 originated from more than 61 countries of the world, with USA topping the list. Constituting about 80.18% of the total inflow, USA, UK, Singapore, South Korea, Hong Kong, Malaysia, India, The Netherlands, Norway, and Sri Lanka are the top 10 source countries of FDI (Table 4.3).

4.2.4. *Trends in trade*

To enhance the trade volume, Bangladesh adopted a market-oriented development strategy and liberalized its external sector policy as per the guidelines of the World Bank and the IMF in the early 1980s. A large number of manufacturing enterprises were returned to former local owners to increase the private sector participation in the economy. Both tariff and non-tariff barriers were substantially reduced in order to accelerate trade liberalization in the country. Gradual changes in Bangladesh's trade policies have led to an increase in its trade volume. Three distinct phases can be identified in Bangladesh's trade policy regimes. The first phase (1972–1975) was distinguished for heavy controls on export and import as well as pervasive price control. The second phase (1976–1990) was marked by a move

Table 4.3: FDI Inflows by Major Sources/Countries (in Million USD)

Country	2015	Percentage of Total FDI
USA	573.77	25.67
UK	300.89	13.46
Singapore	175.27	7.84
South Korea	150.23	6.72
Hong Kong	141.58	6.33
Malaysia	110.46	4.94
India	102.70	4.59
The Netherlands	97.20	4.35
Norway	77.60	3.47
Sri Lanka	62.79	2.81
Others	442.99	19.82

Source: Annual Report 2015, Bank of Bangladesh, p. 34.

toward a market-based economy, beginning of denationalization, modest downward adjustment of tariffs, partial elimination of quantitative restriction, and policy support to the RMG export. The third phase (1990–present) approached trade liberalization in a more concerted manner. Major progress made so far includes substantial scaling down and rationalization of tariffs, removal of trade-related quantitative restriction, unification of exchange rates, and move to a managed floating exchange rate regime. Despite frequent skids from its path, the trade liberalization agenda continues to make overall progress over time (Commonwealth, 2014). As a result of these efforts, the values of export from Bangladesh increased seven-fold in less than 15 years.[2]

Table 4.4 indicates the trends of trade in Bangladesh for the period 2000–2017. The value of trade increased constantly from the year 2000. The trade value, which was only US $15,272 million in 2000, increased to US $88,801 million in 2017. The total trade

---

[2] The period taken is from 1980 to 1995.

Table 4.4: Trends of Total Mercantile Trade
in Bangladesh (Million USD)

Year	Export	Import	Total Trade
2000	6389	8883	15,272
2001	6080	9018	15,098
2002	6149	8592	14,741
2003	6990	10,434	17,424
2004	8305	12,036	20,341
2005	9297	13,889	23,186
2006	11,802	16,034	27,836
2007	12,453	18,596	31,049
2008	15,370	23,860	39,230
2009	15,083	21,833	36,916
2010	19,194	27,821	47,016
2011	24,439	36,214	60,653
2012	25,127	34,173	59,300
2013	29,114	37,085	66,199
2014	30,405	41,119	71,524
2015	32,379	42,047	74,426
2016	34,894	44,832	79,727
2017	35,965	52,836	88,801

Source: UN statistics.

volume doubled during this period. Of the total trade volume, export constitutes 40% while the rest is contributed by import.

The data for the major export destinations of Bangladesh are presented in Table 4.5. It shows that the highest volumes of goods were exported to the USA, followed by other destinations like Germany, UK, and Spain. It is to be noted that RMGs is one of the major export items of Bangladesh and is exported mainly to developed countries like USA and those in EU. It is worth mentioning that the same apparel and clothing sector also attracted the highest amount of FDI. Foreign firms in this sector have contributed immensely to enhance the trade of Bangladesh. Some of the other major export items are animal/vegetable fats, footwear, etc.

Table 4.5: Major Export Destinations During 2015

	Countries	Million USD
1	United States	6139.4
2	Germany	4673.2
3	United Kingdom	3499.9
4	Spain	1845.4
5	France	1755.4
6	Italy	1353.7
7	Canada	1062.6
8	Japan	957.4
9	Belgium	904.5
10	Netherlands	817.5

Source: Authors' calculation based on WITS data.

Table 4.6: Major Import Destinations in 2015

	Countries	Million USD
1	China	10,349.3
2	India	5882.1
3	Singapore	4417.9
4	Hong Kong, China	2624.0
5	Indonesia	2203.6
6	Japan	1704.5
7	Korea, Rep.	1480.6
8	Malaysia	1442.8
9	Brazil	1249.8
10	Kuwait	1196.0

Source: Authors' calculation based on WITS data.

Table 4.6 shows the major import destinations of Bangladesh in 2015. The data show that Bangladesh imported the majority of goods from China, followed by India. It is interesting to note that the import volume from one country is twice that of the other. The import volume from China was US $10 billion, while it was only US $5 billion for India.

It is understood from the details mentioned earlier that the FDI policy in Bangladesh has been more liberal beginning from the early 1980s. Almost all major economic activities have opened up for FDI. Service, chemical, glass and ceramics, and food sector were the major recipient sectors of FDI in Bangladesh. With regard to export, it is apparent that the major goods which are exported by Bangladesh are textiles. It is also a major recipient of FDI. Thus, with respect to this sector, it is obvious that FDI has helped in enhancing Bangladesh's export.

4.3. Bhutan

4.3.1. *Background*

Among the SAARC group of countries, Bhutan is the smallest. The country has brought in a paradigm shift in development theory by introducing a unique concept called Gross National Happiness (GNH) index. This is based on the four pillars of sustainable economic development, preservation and promotion of culture and tradition, conservation of the environment, and good governance.[3] In the last 50 years of planned socio-economic development, the country has progressed from the traditional stage to the precondition stage for economic takeoff. Bhutan has achieved exceptional economic growth over the past three decades. Bhutan's real GDP growth accelerated to 7.99% during 2016–2017, up from the previous year's growth of 6.6%. This was largely driven by impressive performance in the construction and service sectors (including transport, storage, and communications, etc.), reflecting ongoing pre-construction as well as construction works on the new hydropower projects. Among the three broad sectors, the tertiary sector

---

[3] The spirit and intent of this concept as articulated in the Bhutan Vision 2020 document is to "maximize the happiness of all Bhutanese and to enable them to achieve their full and innate potential as human beings."

continuously recorded the highest share in the economy with 42.02% in 2016, followed by the secondary sector at 41.46% and primary sector at 16.52%.

Significant achievements in social development have also been made in recent years, with the number of poor being approximately halved between 2007 and 2012. However, the challenge remains for Bhutan to expand its economic base and make its growth more inclusive, especially for unemployed youth and women.

4.3.2. *FDI policy of Bhutan*

Traditionally, Bhutan pursued a conservative and restrictive foreign investment policy as there were large-scale concerns that FDI may have an undesirable impact on Bhutanese tradition and culture. Thus, there has been a general fear of a large influx of foreign business houses from the neighboring countries. This led to the existence of only a handful of foreign investments in Bhutan (Jigme, 2006). However, since the 1990s, significant liberalization toward opening up of the economy has taken place, with the introduction of customs tariff schedule aimed toward the reduction of customs duty on a range of imports from the third countries. This was followed by Foreign Exchange Regulations, 1997, that removed several restrictions in foreign exchange transactions. At around the same time, several legislations, viz. the Bankruptcy Act, 1999; Movable and Immovable Properties Act, 1999; Companies Act, 2000; Environmental Assessment Act, 2000; Sales Tax, Customs and Excise Act, 2000; Income Tax Act, 2001; Industrial Property Act, 2001; FDI policy, 2002, etc., were enacted and adopted to strengthen the legal framework.

The first flow of foreign investment came to Bhutan by as early as 1971 when State Bank of India (SBI) invested 40% equity in Royal Bank of Bhutan (RBOB) to develop the banking sector in the country. A clear-cut policy initiative by the Royal Government of Bhutan toward attracting foreign investment came with the announcement of the FDI Policy 2002. It acknowledged the beneficial role of FDI on the country — through employment creation, provision of capital and technology, the introduction of new management skills, greater access to international market, earning of convertible foreign exchange, and the provision of wider opportunities and broader choices to the Bhutanese people.[4] For effective implementation of the FDI Policy 2002, the Foreign Direct Investment Rules and Regulations, 2005 was brought out by the Ministry of Trade & Industry. It was decided that the minimum size of the investment shall be $1 million in the manu-facturing sector (Mineral Processing, Agriculture and Agro-processing, Forestry and Wood-based Industries, Livestock-based Industries, Light Industries including Electronic Industries, Engineering and Power-Intensive Industries) and $0.5 million in the service sector (Tourism including Hotels, Transport Services, Roads and Bridges, Education, Business Infrastructure, Information Technology, Financial Services, Housing); in either case, the foreign investor can hold up to 70% of the equity. The initial debt/equity ratio of the foreign direct investment business shall not exceed a 1:1 ratio. All commercial undertakings are, therefore, required to obtain a license from the Ministry of Trade & Industry, as contained in the General Guidelines for Industrial and Commercial Ventures in Bhutan, 1997.

The FDI Policy 2002 succeeded in getting approval of foreign capital from two international hospitality chains — US $20 million from Bhutan Resorts Corporation Limited, a joint venture between the Bhutan Tourism Corporation Limited and the International Group of Amman Resorts, and another multimillion investment from Bhutan Eco Ventures Limited, a joint venture between the Bhutan International Company and M/S HPL Leisure Properties (West Asia) Private Limited of Singapore. Both commenced their operations sometime in 2004. Besides the hospitality sector, Bhutan also witnessed FDI inflow in the beverage industry segment in the form of franchise, technical, and operational support.[5]

The FDI policy further liberalized with the adoption of the New FDI Policy in 2010 which was further amended during July and December 2014. FDI Policy 2010 was laid down in line with the objectives of

---

[4] Foreign Direct Investment Policy 2002, Royal Government of Bhutan.

[5] Bhutan Beverages Company Ltd was established in 2002 after signing a franchise agreement with Coca-Cola Company Limited and Tashi Group of companies.

Economic Development Policy 2010. The amendment allowed FDI in other activities with maximum foreign investors' equity of 74% and a minimum project cost of Nu 50 million and Nu 25 million for manufacturing and services, respectively, listed under the schedule I and II FDI policy.

4.3.3. *Trends in FDI inflows*

The share of FDI in the GDP of Bhutan remains relatively low as compared to other developing countries. The FDI stock constitutes less than 10% of the GDP. In South Asia, Bhutan attracts the least volume of FDI. In 2016, FDI inflow was outpaced by divestment, resulting in a negative inflow of US $12.5 million (UNCTAD, 2017). This is done in order to protect its culture and environment, and geographical factors hold back the region in many economic issues. In addition, FDI development is limited by a substantially controlled system and an inadequate policy in the areas of industrial license, trade, work, and finance. The shortage of skilled labor also acts as a major hindrance to development. Bhutan is ranked 73rd out of 190 countries in the World Bank's 2017 Doing Business Report. For a small landlocked country, this ranking is nevertheless satisfactory.

The Government of Bhutan has been among the most active in South Asia in terms of introducing reforms, creating public information and credit register, and simplifying the procedures necessary for business establishment. In early 2015, the government relaxed FDI regulations, and foreign investors are now able to buy land. The pharmaceutical sector is now open to FDI. A measure has been introduced which makes it easier to exchange local currency for foreign currencies. For several years, FDI has been rising steadily; however it still remains weak. A railway project linking Bhutan to Bengal, India, has been planned, which could help increase the FDI flows from this neighboring state of Bhutan. The Government of Bhutan wishes to continue restricting FDI in certain sectors in order to avoid competition with local traders.

The hydroelectric energy production sector is, to a certain degree, threatened by the melting of glaciers, which represents a growing threat. However, along with the construction sector, it remains the most attractive to investment, which mostly comes from India. Better management of sightseeing tours and better air service could benefit the tourism sector, which at the moment contributes only marginally to GDP, despite its recent growth. Lastly, the agriculture and manufacturing sectors receive too little FDI.[6]

The trend in the FDI inflows in Bhutan is depicted in Figure 4.2. The total FDI inflow which was only US $2.4 million in 2002 has increased to more than US $7 million in the year 2016. It is noticeable that in the years 2006 and 2010 the FDI inflow was the highest at US $72.2 and $78.5 million, respectively. This is mainly due to the investment made by Ferro Silicon, an Indian company, in 2006 and by another Indian investment in the financial sector in 2010. The name of this investor was not available.

FDI flows into Bhutan have picked up in the last few years. There were a total of 22 approved FDI joint ventures as of 2010–2011, 12 of which are currently under construction and 10 are operational, targeting tourism, manufacturing, and IT sectors (Table 4.7).

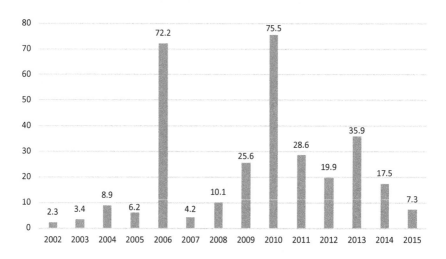

Figure 4.2: FDI Inflows in Bhutan (Million USD)

Source: Authors' calculation based on UN stat data.

---

[6] See Bhutan Foreign Investment retrieved from https://en.portal.santandertrade.com/establish-overseas/bhutan/investing-3, accessed on 12 May 2018.

Table 4.7:   Details on FDI-Approved Projects in Bhutan (Million Nu)

Year	Countries	Activity/ Sectors	No. of Projects	Value	Status
Approved before FDI Policy was implemented	India	Financial Services	1	201.62	Operating
	Virgin Islands	Hotel Services	1	563	Operating
	Singapore	Tourism Services	1	375	Operating
2006	Sri Lanka	Specialty Fats	1	129.32	Closed Down
	India	Ferro Silicon	1	308.48	Operating
	UK	Specialty Fats	1	180	Dropped
	Denmark	Security Services	1	30.58	Operating
2007	India	Steel/Calcium Carbide	2	454.74	Under Construction/ Operational
	Sri Lanka	Jewelry	1	44.12	Dropped
	Kazakhstan	VSAT and Broadband Internet Services	1	198.8	Dropped
2008	India	Manufacturing	2	1198.28	Under Construction/ Operational
	USA & UK	Hotel	1	114.63	Under Construction
	Germany	Silicon Carbide	1	1123.22	Under Construction
2009	Thailand	Hotel Services	1	41.84	Under Construction
	Singapore	IT Park Development	1	225.373	Under Construction
	India	Dairy and Agro Products	1	324.6	Under Construction

(*Continued*)

Table 4.7:   (*Continued*)

Year	Countries	Activity/ Sectors	No. of Projects	Value	Status
2010	India	Banking	1	300.00	Operating
	India	Plaster of Paris/Steel	2	848.61	Under Construction/ Operational
	Singapore	Hotel Services	1	71.30	Under Construction
	USA	Hotel Services	1	90.03	Operating
2011	India	Power	1	8160	Under Construction
	Singapore	Hotel Services	1	380	Under Construction
	Samoa	Hotel Services	1	604.17	Under Construction

Source: Department of Industry, Ministry of Economic Affairs, Royal Government of Bhutan.

An additional four FDI joint ventures — two from Sri Lanka and one each from the United Kingdom and Kazakhstan — were approved but dropped midway. As exhibited in Table 4.6 and Figures 4.3 and 4.4, the major investments (around 80% of total investment) have come from India, followed by Germany (8.4%) and Singapore (5.1%). Sector-wise, an unprecedented 60% investment is concentrated in a single power project — Dagachhu Hydro Power Corporation Ltd. — promoted by the Asian Development Bank and the first Public–Private Partnership (PPP) project in Bhutan with the Druk Green Power Corporation (DGPC), Tata Power, and the National Pension Fund as joint venture partners.

Other sectors of prominence include manufacturing (around 13%), financial services (10%), and hotel services (9%). It is interesting to note that in each year of our reference period, India has invested in Bhutan. The major sectors where Indian investors have invested in Bhutan are Financial Services, Manufacturing, Wholesale Trading, and Power. Indian banks like Punjab National Bank and

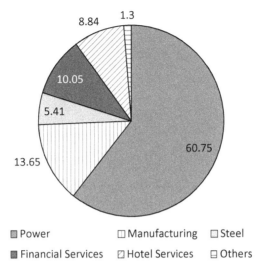

Figure 4.3:   Distribution of FDI in Bhutan: Across Sectors (up to 2011–2012) by Value of Projects (%)

Source: Authors' calculation based on the Department of Industry, Ministry of Economic Affairs, Royal government of Bhutan data.

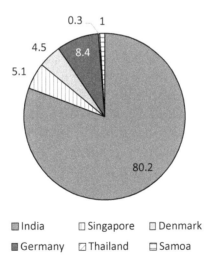

Figure 4.4:   Distribution of FDI in Bhutan from Countries (up to 2011–2012) by Value of Projects (%)

Source: Department of Industry, Ministry of Economic Affairs, Royal Government of Bhutan.

State Bank of India have made a huge investment in Bhutan's financial sector. To a large extent, the country is highly dependent on India for cheaper unskilled labor as well as skills and technology.

4.3.4. *Trends in trade*

Though Bhutanese trade has been flourishing since the 19th century, it received added impetus in the 20th century. There has been massive diversification in the trade of Bhutan in the last decade. Trade diversification reflects an economy's growing competitiveness resulting from its broadening productive base, with processes getting more efficient, improving fundamentals, and its increasing willingness and capabilities to effectively integrate with the world economy. Both export and import values of the country have increased tremendously in our reference period.

Table 4.8 shows the trend in the trade volume of Bhutan. A constantly increasing trend can be noticed. The value of the trade which was only US $278 million in 2000 increased to US $1590 million in 2017. There was a fivefold increase in the volume of the trade. The highest volume of trade took place in 2011. The value of trade in 2011 was US $1711 million.

The data in Table 4.9 reveal the major goods exported by Bhutan in the year 2015. Iron and steel were top products exported in that year. The total value of the export was more than $168 million. It was followed by Electrical machinery, Salt, and Copper. It is important to note that despite being an agriculturally dominated economy, all the major export goods from Bhutan are manufacturing goods.

The major goods imported by Bhutan in 2015 are depicted in Table 4.10. The data show that Nuclear reactors and boilers were the top goods imported by Bhutan. Like the major items exported, all major products imported are also manufacturing goods. One can observe that Iron and steel and Electrical machinery, and equipment, and their parts are both in the list of top goods exported and imported. This implies that Bhutan is importing raw iron and exporting the finished and value-added iron.

Table 4.8: Total Mercantile Trade by Bhutan

Year	Total Trade (EX+IM) (Million USD)
2000	278
2001	297
2002	309
2003	382
2004	594
2005	644
2006	834
2007	1200
2008	1065
2009	1025
2010	1495
2011	1718
2012	1527
2013	1453
2014	1515
2015	1610
2016	1527
2017	1590

Source: UN stat.

Table 4.9:   Major Goods Exported by Bhutan in 2015

S. No.	Products	Export Value (Thousand USD)
1.	Iron and steel	168,434.2
2.	Electrical machinery, equipment, and their parts	71,961.6
3.	Salt, Sulfur, earth and stone	61,243.3
4.	Copper and articles thereof	43,405.5
5.	Inorganic chemicals and compounds of precious metals	31,395.4

Source: Authors' calculation based on WITS data.

Table 4.10:   Major Goods Imported by Bhutan in 2015

S. No.	Products	Import Value (000 USD)
1.	Nuclear reactors and boilers	160,798.7
2.	Mineral fuels, oils and product	159,411.5
3.	Vehicles of railway/tramway roll-stock	142,182.0
4.	Iron and steel	94,464.0
5.	Electrical machinery, equipment, and their parts	60,579.2

Source: Authors' calculation based on WITS data.

Leaving behind the traditional and conservative FDI policy, Bhutan liberalized its economy in the 1990s. Since then, a large amount of FDI has flowed into Bhutan. India has been the largest investor in Bhutan, accounting for around 80% of the total FDI inflows. Hospitality and power generation sectors were found to be the highest recipients of FDI. This is because of the reason that Bhutan is endowed with natural water resources.

4.4. India

4.4.1. *Background*

The Indian economy continues to be one of the fastest growing economies in the world. At the current exchange rate, it is the 12th largest economy in the world. But in terms of purchasing power parity, the Indian economy ranks the fourth largest in the world.[7] The Indian growth story began with the introduction of the New Economic Policy in 1991. It was with the introduction of reforms that the values of FDI jumped from $7 billion in 2008 to more than US $60 billion in 2017. GDP values have also increased from $834 billion in 2008 to US $2611 billion in 2017. After a few quarters of downturn following the global economic meltdown, the Indian economy has again started showing an impressive growth trend in recent quarters.

---

[7] IMF and IFS online statistics.

Although industrial production has been showing a double-digit growth trend, the core industrial sector, which is growing slower than the GDP growth rate, may hinder capacity building and the overall growth in the future. But the unprecedented inflation rate remains a major threat for sustainable growth (Mukherjee and Sinha, 2011).

Although economic reforms began in India in the early 1980s, a comprehensive liberalization and privatization process started only in July 1991 against the backdrop of the BoP crisis. For attracting FDI, many policies have been introduced in India. Major initiatives such as industrial decontrol, simplification of investment procedures, enactment of competition law, liberalization of trade policy, full commitment to safeguarding intellectual property rights, financial sector reforms, liberalization of exchange rate regulations, etc., have been taken. In the last 3 years, the government has eased 87 FDI rules across 21 sectors to accelerate economic growth and boost jobs (Ray, 2017). This has provided a liberal, attractive, and investor-friendly investment climate.

Another important and historical step taken by the government was the introduction of the Goods and Service Tax (GST). GST has clubbed 18 different taxes levied at various levels. Some of them were federal while some were provincial taxes. GST enormously helped the logistics companies to reduce their cost and time consumed in ferrying goods from one place to another. All these above measures have played a vital role in elevating India in the ranking of Doing Business index 2018.

4.4.2. *FDI policy in India*

There has been a continuous change in the government's approach to FDI since 1947. Because it is a resource-poor economy, especially in capital resources, India was always receptive to foreign investment. The foreign exchange crisis of 1957–1958 led to further liberalization of the government's approach toward FDI (Kumar, 2003). However, the government adopted a more restrictive attitude toward FDI in the late 1960s as local industries developed. In 1973, the new Foreign Exchange Regulation Act (FERA) came into force, requiring all foreign companies operating in India to register under Indian corporate legislation with up to 40% equity (Kumar, 2003).

In the 1980s, India brought about some historical changes in its FDI policy. FDI was now considered as a source to earn foreign exchange reserves rather than act as a supplement to local industries. The low productivity and inefficiency of local industries were considered to be an outcome of overprotection provided to Indian industries from the international market. Such protection made Indian industries inefficient as compared to other developing countries which were having liberal FDI policies. The policies on FDI in India were reformed by introducing liberal measures.

In 1991, India adopted the New Economic Policy. Since then, the Indian economy has undergone systematic changes from a highly state-controlled regime to a more liberal and outward-oriented market-friendly regime. A series of measures were gradually initiated to improve productivity and quality and to reduce the cost of production (Choudhury, 2018). An important reform was the abolition of restriction imposed on foreign industries by FERA. The public sector was freed from a number of constraints and was provided greater autonomy. The service sector was opened to foreign direct investors — mainly Real Estate, Telecommunications, and Banking sector. Over the years, a series of policy measures were announced to liberalize the FDI environment in the country. Gradually, almost all the sectors have been opened for foreign investment inflows. As a result, India today has one of the most attractive FDI policies in the South Asian region (Sahoo, 2006).

4.4.3. *Trends in FDI inflows*

From Figure 4.5, an increasing trend can be noticed in the total inflow of FDI in India from 2000 to 2017. The effect of the global economic meltdown on the FDI inflows to India can be clearly noticed after 2008. The pace of investment reduced by a large volume; however, it has started rising again since 2014.

Table 4.11 shows the major countries from where FDI has flowed into India during the year 2016 are Mauritius, Singapore,

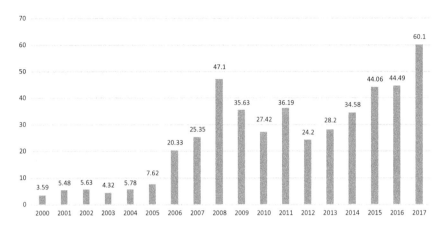

Figure 4.5: Trends in FDI Inflows in India (Billion USD)

Source: Authors' calculation based on UN stat data.

Table 4.11: Major Countries Investing in India (Million USD)

Country	2000–2012	2013	2014	2015	2016
Mauritius	71,808.95	5722.39	7073.12	9242.8	15,069.46
Singapore	18,792.53	3874.14	7092.38	13,414.32	9822.18
USA	11,111.90	771.90	1663.45	3855.7	2621.2
UK	17,103.65	3606.48	1096.32	920.45	1660.86
The Netherlands	8468.13	2112.94	3253.58	3003.32	2996.17
Japan	14,019.20	142073	2335.02	1739.42	5781.17
Cyprus	6799.76	469.6	657.39	517.52	667.40
Germany	5133.46	1014.86	1151.57	1144.47	1102.76
France	3407.21	441.37	612.07	428.77	650.19
UAE	2362.04	283.94	279.28	521.8	1196.82

Source: DIPP, Government of India.

USA, and UK, with Mauritius accounting for more than 32% of the total FDI inflow followed by Singapore. Service sector (both financial and non-financial) has attracted the highest amount of FDI. It is followed by computer and telecommunication services, which managed to attract 8% of FDI each in the same time period.

4.4.4. *Trends in trade*

Since 1991, the government of India adopted the policy of economic liberalization, privatization, and globalization to increase international trade in India. Devaluation of the Indian rupee in 1991 and the convertibility of Indian rupee in trade account during 1993–1994 and 1994–1995, respectively, improved the balance of trade position in 1993–1994 with a value of INR –33.50 billion. Figure 4.6 represents India's foreign trade since 1991.

Figure 4.6 illustrates that the overall gap between export and import has increased, and this leads to a widening trade deficit of India. The trade deficit of India widened to INR –10,348.44 billion in 2012–2013 which was highest from 1991–1992 to 2016–2017. According to the ministry of commerce, this trade deficit widens largely due to lower demand in the United States and European markets created by the global financial crisis in these two major trade partners of India. After 2012–2013, Indian's trade balance improved as the country's exports crossed ₹19,050.11 billion in 2013–2014 while its import in the same financial year amounted to ₹27,154.34

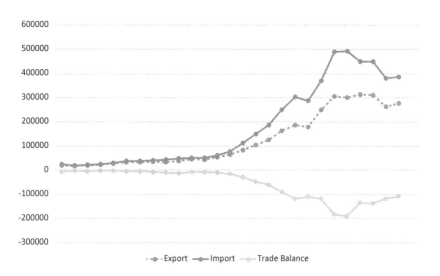

Figure 4.6:   India's Foreign Trade After 1991

Source: Reserve Bank of India, Handbook of Statistics on Indian Economy.

billion. Between 2015–2016 and 2016–2017, India's trade balance further declined due to a decrease in India's imports as the government in recent years has been focusing on domestic production through some programs like "Make in India" and others. From 2015–2016 to 2016–2017, India's imports declined from ₹24,902.98 billion to ₹25,668.20 billion. According to the trading economies dataset, India's trade balance reflects sustained trade deficits since 1980 mostly due to robust growth in imports, particularly of mineral fuels, oils and waxes, and bituminous substances and pearls, precious and semi-precious stones, and jewelry. In recent years, the largest trade deficits were documented with China, Switzerland, Saudi Arabia, Iraq, and Indonesia. India records trade surpluses with the US, United Arab Emirates, Hong Kong, United Kingdom, and Vietnam.

4.4.5. *Direction of India's foreign trade*

India's direction of foreign trade from 2012–2013 to 2016–2017 reveals the major sources of Indian import and major destinations of Indian exports are across the globe. It is evident from the data that both export and import values have increased continuously from all the country groups. There has been significant market diversification in India's trade. Region-wise, while India's exports to Europe and America declined, its exports to Asia and Africa have increased. The data show that the major sources of Indian exports are OPEC countries followed by the European Union. Petroleum products which are sourced from OPEC countries are the primary reason for this group to be top in the list. India imports raw petroleum products, and because of low labor cost these raw petroleum products are processed in India and again exported back to another destination. Therefore, India's trade basket contains petroleum products on both the import and export side at the top. Developing countries have also emerged as major trading partners of India in recent times. Asian countries like China, Taiwan, and Hong Kong are the major contributors in the developing country group.

4.5. Nepal

4.5.1. *Background*

Nepal is among the poorest countries in the world, with approximately 25% of its population living below the poverty line. The agricultural sector still forms the backbone of the Nepalese economy. An isolated, agrarian economy until the mid-20th century, the country has, however, made progress toward sustainable economic growth since the 1950s and is committed to a program of economic liberalization. Tourism represents a small but expanding industry. Foreign tourism is primarily confined to the Kathmandu Valley, which is the only area equipped with the necessary hotels, food supplies, roads, and international transport services. Nepal is heavily dependent on remittances, which amount to as much as 30% of the GDP. Agriculture is the mainstay of the economy, providing a livelihood for almost two-thirds of the population but accounting for only one-third of the GDP. Industrial activity mainly involves the processing of agricultural products, including pulses, jute, sugarcane, tobacco, and grain.

In 2017, Nepal's GDP was around $78.55 billion while it was $12.5 billion in 2009. Notably, 27% of the GDP comes from agriculture, 13.5% from industry, and the rest from the service sector. Of late, growth in the service sector is noticeable. Labor force consists of 18 million people, and 75% of them work in the agricultural sector. Nepal still suffers from high-level unemployment (46% in 2010) and high-level inflation of 9–10%.

4.5.2. *FDI policy*

A proper and clear-cut policy toward foreign investment was introduced in Nepal for the first time in the early 1980s, with the enactment of the Investment and Industrial Enterprise Act of 1987. In its pursuit of outward-oriented policies, Nepal started encouraging private foreign investment in every industrial sector (medium and large scale). However, in sectors like defence activities were there was restriction of foreign investment. Joint ventures were the most preferred form of investment. The Foreign Investment and Technology Transfer Act (FITTA) 1992 governs foreign investment. This offers equal treatment to foreign investment companies. Technology transfer is possible in all sectors of industries, repatriation is guaranteed in foreign currency, business/residential visa for investors is available, and there is clear provision of dispute settlement.

In the case of medium-sized industries, foreign equity holding of 50% was allowed. In large industries which were exporting more than 90% of their total production, foreign equity was allowed even up to 100%. In other large industries, the maximum foreign investment limit was set at 80% foreign equity. Foreign investors were required to take formal approval from the Foreign Investment Promotion Division, the Ministry of Industry. With a view to encouraging FDI, Nepal announced a new set of incentives through the 1987 Act, under which the full remittance of dividends was allowed. Further, foreign workers were allowed to be brought in when nationals were not available. A 5-year tax holiday on profits was also allowed, and this was later extended to 10 years. Importers were allowed to import their inputs without paying any duty, either through a duty drawback or bonded warehouse facility. One of the objectives of Nepal's Ninth Five-Year Plan (1997–2002) was to ensure the safe entry of foreign capital, technology, and managerial and technical skills particularly for the development of industry, tourism, water resources, and infrastructure; to accelerate the process of industrialization through mobilization of foreign investment and private sector participation; and to promote export in the international market by improving production, productivity, and quality.

In 2015, the country adopted a new constitution that embraces Nepal as a multiparty democratic federal republic with the private sector-led liberal economy. The government is committed to the promotion of foreign investment and has enacted and amended various investment-related and sector-specific laws to provide a unique opportunity for FDI in Nepal. Although Nepal is currently classified as a least developed country (LDC) by the United Nations, its goal is to graduate from this status by 2022 and transition to a middle-income country by 2030. Very recently, during 2018, Nepal announced its latest investment guide which lays down detailed procedures to invest in Nepal.

4.5.3. *Trends in FDI inflows*

The trend in FDI inflows in Nepal is presented in Figure 4.7. A minimum amount of FDI inflows can be noticed up to 2009. However, after 2009 FDI inflows showed an increasing trend. Nepal received more than 100 million of FDI during 2016, and this was the maximum volume in Nepal's history.

Table 4.12 shows the approved FDI stock with regard to its country of origin along with yearly approval for the last 3 years. Though FDI is flowing from several countries, India stands out as the most important source. It is also noteworthy that investment from China is increasing significantly in recent years. In total stock, China ranks second after India, followed by the USA, Japan, and Korea. South Asia occupies almost 44% of Nepalese FDI in terms of value.

Bangladesh has mostly invested in management training, restaurant, and agro-based products. On the other hand, Sri Lanka has invested in advertisement and media industries. China's initial

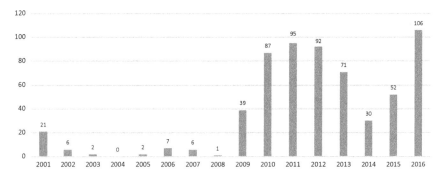

Figure 4.7:   Trends of FDI Inflows in Nepal (Million USD)

Source: Authors' calculation based on UN stat data.

Table 4.12:   Values and Industries Approved for FDI by Country of Origin (Million NR)

Country of Origin	Up to 2009–2010 No. of Industries	Up to 2009–2010 Value of Approved Foreign Investment	Up to 2009–2010 Total Employment	2007–2008 No. of Industries	2007–2008 Value	2008–2009 No. of Industries	2008–2009 Value	2009–2010 No. of Industries	2009–2010 Value
Australia	29	356.82	826	5	17.48			5	26.05
Bangladesh	23	254.86	4033	1	5	4	20.5	2	4.45
Bhutan	3	3.61	98						
Brazil	3	504.43	471			1	500		
Canada	21	2133.04	1795	2	11.4	2	41.73	2	1403.4
China	332	5848.77	20259	15	231.3	51	875.24	58	715.75
Denmark	18	144.36	846	1	5	3	62.3	2	12.5
France	43	271.3	1829	1	7	4	14.1		
Germany	75	898.82	3759	8	54.3	3	69	4	11.6
Hong Kong	18	692.84	2554	1	30			1	20
India	462	25,381.45	53,101	29	3645.4	28	2341.31	27	3993.56
Japan	146	1140.49	6450	5	11.25	6	33.17	4	20.2
Mauritius	3	2445	723					2	2080
Netherlands	32	526.12	2584	3	15.97	2	16.5	3	10.7
Norway	11	1129.83	676	2	54.5			1	4
Pakistan	15	149.73	2403	1	5	1	2.4		

(*Continued*)

Table 4.12:   (*Continued*)

Country of Origin	Up to 2009–2010			2007–2008		2008–2009		2009–2010	
	No. of Industries	Value of Approved Foreign Investment	Total Employment	No. of Industries	Value	No. of Industries	Value	No. of Industries	Value
South Korea	131	4245.34	5863	17	2898.84	5	72	20	174.41
Singapore	21	961.39	1687			4	564.5	2	12.5
Sri Lanka	3	**37.41**	**83**						
Switzerland	30	324.85	605			2	163.2		
Taiwan	9	174.62	596						
UAE	4	883.37	661	1	403.37			1	400
UK	94	1479.04	7609	11	318.22	10	161.94	6	21.5
USA	166	4874.5	12,034	9	81.98	8	44	10	51.3
Others	206	3135.68	12,968	27	172.09	16	373.65	21	138.08
SAARC	506	25,827.06	59,718	31	3655.4	33	2364.21	29	3998.01
SAARC % of Total	**26.66**	**44.53**	**41.32**	**22.30**	**45.88**	**22.00**	**44.15**	**16.96**	**43.93**
Total	1898	57,997.67	144,513	139	7968.1	150	5355.54	171	9100

Source: Industrial Statistics (various years), Department of Industry, Government of Nepal.

investment was mainly in construction and housing sectors, but by 2010 China entered into many other areas including hotel and res-taurants, telecom, publishing, gold mining, and extraction industries. Taken together, India is a major investor in all sectors.

The majority of this investment has been in the manufacturing sector followed by the service and tourism sector. Among the manu-facturing industries, the textile sector including RMGs, chemicals, plastic, food, beverage, tobacco, fabricated metal sectors, etc. are the main industries which have attracted foreign investment.

4.5.4. *Trends in trade*

Like any other country, trade is one of the most important compo-nents of the Nepalese economy. Currently, the total foreign trade ratio to GDP is around 37%. Compared to the average growth rate of total trade at 16.1%, the average growth rates of export and import are 1.0% and 20.4%, respectively, during 2004–2015, clearly indicating that imports have tended to grow more signifi-cantly as compared to exports. After the accession of Nepal to the WTO, the share of its export in total trade decreased from 28.2% in 2004–2005 to 14.5% in 2015–2016 in comparison to the increase in import from 71.8% to 85.9% during the same period. The big gap between export and import is generating huge trade deficit as well as creating foreign exchange burden to the economy. The total value of the imports of one product, viz. petroleum products, is greater than the total value of all the commodities exported. The trend in Nepal is presented in Table 4.13. The data show the value of trade which was only $2377 million in 2000 and increased to $11,250 million in 2017. The data reveal that Iron and steel, Carpets, and other textile floor materials are major export items of Nepal. Nepal majorly imports mineral oil and fuels and other finished goods.

Even though Nepal liberalized its economy in the early 1980s, it has attracted only a few FDI projects till date. Since 2009, Nepal has experienced an increase in its FDI inflows. India, China, and Germany are the major investors in Nepal. Agriculture, food, and beverages are the major recipient sectors of FDI. Nepal exported

Table 4.13: Trends of Total
Mercantile Trade in Nepal
(Million USD)

Year	Trade Value (EX+IM)
2000	2377
2001	2210
2002	1987
2003	2416
2004	2709
2005	3147
2006	3330
2007	3990
2008	4529
2009	5207
2010	5989
2011	6693
2012	6977
2013	7450
2014	8450
2015	7372
2016	9631
2017	11,250

Source: UN stat.

large volumes of carpets and other floor materials and imported mineral fuels and iron and steel.

4.6. Sri Lanka

4.6.1. *Background*

Sri Lanka, a small island nation located in the South Asian region, had a GDP of $278.415 billion and a per capita GDP of about $4,085 (PPP) in 2017. Despite having the potential of emerging as a global maritime transport hub due to locational advantage, the economic growth in Sri Lanka has been subject to fluctuations owing to several internal and external factors in the past. The country has however witnessed a relatively stronger growth regime in recent years. While the average GDP growth rate in the country over the 1991–2000 period was 5.22%, the same during the 2003–2008 period increased to 6.34%. The integration of the Sri Lankan economy with the world economy is getting deeper, though the export of goods and services expressed as a percentage of GDP has declined to some extent in recent years. The closer association of the Sri Lankan economy with the global economy is reflected with its GDP declining to around 4% in 2009 in the aftermath of the economic recession.

The Sri Lankan economy is much more advanced compared to its South Asian counterparts such as Bangladesh, Bhutan, and Pakistan in terms of the human and social capital index. Owing to a strong government which is focused on primary and secondary education, the literacy rate in Sri Lanka in recent years has crossed 90%. However, the continuance of the civil war in the country spanning over two decades curbed the domestic growth capability on one hand and resulted in less potential foreign participation on the other. The Sri Lankan economy faced the challenges of bankruptcy in 2001 when its debt burden reached around 101% of its GDP. However, better government response to the crisis through newer reform measures and IMF support helped Sri Lanka significantly restore investors' confidence. At present, the Sri Lankan stock market is recognized as one of the best performers in the world. Taking into account its recent past, Sri Lanka has made remarkable progress in various fronts of the economy.

4.6.2. *FDI policy*

FDI inflows have occupied a special place in the development policy of Sri Lanka since the late 1970s, and the linkage has been strengthened further through subsequent reforms. The country has been an attractive location for foreign investment owing to the availability of abundant land resources, skilled labor at relatively lower wage rate, its location along maritime transport routes, strategic access to Indian market, etc. With gradual reforms, Sri Lanka's investment regime has now ensured greater openness to foreigners, barring certain sectors, where investment is either subject to non-automatic approval, or is reserved for Sri Lankan nationals.

The gradual FDI policy reforms in Sri Lanka have ensured relaxation of restrictions on foreign participation, with deeper entry permitted in a greater number of sectors. BOI was created during the early stage of the reform process to function as a single-window facilitation point for investors, and its responsibilities include approving proposals, establishing eligibility for tax incentives, administering export-processing zones and industrial parks, etc. BOI has contributed significantly to lowering transaction costs of investing in the country. FDI entry in Sri Lanka during 1990s suffered from several factors including customs clearing procedures, land-related problems associated with building factories, and infrastructure issues (World Trade Organization, 2004). The stream of policy reforms since 2000 attempted to address these areas of concern. National Treatment is currently provided to foreign investors, and like local players, they are entitled to receive the applicable incentives provided by the BOI or other relevant authorities. FDI has entered Sri Lanka in all three sectors of the economy, namely, agriculture, manufacturing, and services.

Sri Lanka has communicated to the WTO that its investment regime does not incorporate clauses like local-content requirements, trade-balancing requirements, foreign exchange balancing requirements, exchange restrictions, etc., which might have adverse implications.[8] Sri Lanka has entered into Double Taxation Avoidance Agreement (DTAA) and Bilateral Investment Protection Agreement (BIPA) with several countries for attracting investment from these locations.

Since its establishment, BOI has been offering incentives as a strategy to attract FDI. As per the powers vested by said law, the

---

[8] WTO document G/TRIMS/N/1/LKA/1, 31 March 2000. Noted from WTO (2004).

BOI could deviate from the laws and acts stipulated in Schedule B of the BOI Act including the Inland Revenue law, Customs Ordinance and Exchange Control Act. Accordingly, the BOI granted investment incentives including tax holidays, tax concessions, and exemptions from Customs Ordinance and Exchange Control laws for qualified investments. The BOI exercised its authority under the BOI Law until 2011, and in 2012 BOI Inland Revenue tax concessions were amalgamated and the BOI followed the same tax concessions granted under the Inland Revenue Act thereafter. In 2017, the government introduced a new Inland Revenue Act after consultation with IMF, allowing Sri Lanka to increase government revenue from direct taxes. Instead of providing traditional tax holidays for investments, Sri Lanka has moved to a new incentive regime with the introduction of the new Inland Revenue Act. Accordingly, investors will be granted Incentives by way of Accelerated Depreciation Allowance (ADA) and Tax Credits (TCs) based on the investments made on depreciable assets (UNESCAP[9]).

4.6.3. *Trends in FDI inflows*

There is a long list of counties who have invested in Sri Lanka in recent years. The BOI shows that the investment has come from various countries across the globe, though the statistics is not available for the later years. During 2007–2012, Malaysia was the leading investing country in the Sri Lankan economy. In the year 2007, Malaysia invested $99 million in Sri Lanka, which increased to $164 million in 2009. However, in the year 2010, India emerged as the top investor country for Sri Lanka with an FDI inflow level of $110.23 million, pushing Malaysia to the second position. Apart from India and Malaysia, considerable investments have also come from countries like Hong Kong, UK, Japan, Germany, and Singapore. FDI from China has shown an increasing trend in recent years. South

---

[9]Changes and Developments of Foreign Direct Investment Policy 2016–2017. Retrieved from http://www.unescap.org/sites/default/files/Investment%20Policy%20-%20Sri%20Lanka-%20Recent%20Changes.pdf.

Asian investment in Sri Lanka has however been limited. From 2005 to 2010, the FDI in Sri Lanka from Bangladesh, India, Maldives, Nepal, and Pakistan was $0.94 million, $401.67 million, $5.32 million, $0.14 million, and $4.02 million, respectively. Expressed as a percentage of total FDI inflows in Sri Lanka, the inward FDI from SAARC countries over 2006–2010 stands at 11.35%.

The total FDI (US $1,391 million) received in 2013 was distributed among different sectors, such as US $360 million in the Manufacturing sector, US $236 million in the Service sector, US $787 million in the Infrastructure sector, and US $8 million in the Agriculture sector. This remarkable achievement was made possible by the government's strategies to attract quality investments, which include strengthening Sri Lanka's environment-friendly business climate for existing industries to fill gaps throughout the economic value chain. The domestic investment inflow in 2013 was US $512 million, a sign of confidence of the local investors in the country's ability to prosper in businesses. This is also in line with the government's continued drive to actively promote domestic investments as outlined in Mahinda Chintana — Vision for the Future (BOI, 2013).[10]

Figure 4.8 shows the trend in the FDI inflows in Sri Lanka from 2000 to 2016. The data show that the value of the FDI inflow increased constantly from 2000 to 2008. The values decreased in 2009 and 2010; however, from 2011 they show an increasing trend with the exception of 2015.

Table 4.14 shows the distribution of major sectors attracting FDI in Sri Lanka. It is observed from the table that the infrastructure sector (telecom, power generation, etc.) and manufacturing sector (textile, chemicals, rubber, etc.) are among the major recipients of foreign investment.

Among the South Asian partners, Indian firms have been investing in Sri Lanka for a long time. For instance, an assembly plant for sewing machines was set up by the Shriram group at Ratmalana,

---

[10] Board of Investment, Sri Lanka. Retrieved from http://www.investsrilanka.com/images/publications/pdf/Annual_Report_2013.pdf.

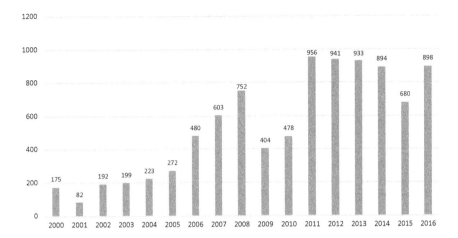

Figure 4.8:   Trends in FDI Inflows in Sri Lanka (Million USD)

Source: Authors' calculation based on UN stat data.

Table 4.14:   Foreign Direct Investment of BOI Enterprise (2007–2012) by Sector (Million USD)

Sector	FDI					
	2007	2008	2009	2010	2011	2012
Manufacturing	135.321	234.777	174.016	189.183	164.470	159.653
Food, Beverages, and Tobacco	29.382	34.100	25.932	14.742	11.338	17.542
Textile, Wearing Apparel, and Leather	47.278	103.479	62.600	72.281	51.398	37.559
Wood and Wooden Products	0.916	4.392	0.769	2.208	1.693	1.430
Paper, Paper Products, and Printing	8.156	0.760	0.000	0.858	20.773	8.713
Chemicals, Petroleum, Coal, and Plastics	4.305	10.890	1.140	5.248	1.754	28.018
Rubber Products	15.831	32.267	47.897	34.679	13.644	16.383
Electronics and Electricals	5.901	6.875	7.669	14.605	23.153	7.863

(Continued)

Table 4.14:   (*Continued*)

Sector	FDI					
	2007	2008	2009	2010	2011	2012
Non-metallic and Mineral Products	5.901	5.266	4.712	12.769	11.178	10.495
Fabricated Metal and Machinery	15.337	14.078	12.544	14.383	14.035	14.913
Other Manufactured Products (not elsewhere specified)	2.314	22.670	10.753	17.410	15.504	16.737
Agriculture	0.473	0.672	0.417	2.652	3.689	6.448
Horticulture and Cultivation of Fruits and Vegetables	0.473	0.672	0.417	2.652	3.689	6.448
Infrastructure	140.957	329.560	526.470	660.821	381.536	305.664
Housing, Property Development and Shopping, and Office complexes	13.433	58.321	30.157	19.864	17.740	42.059
Telephone and Telecommunication Network	111.740	263.426	403.632	553.097	296.064	205.164
Power Generation	15.784	7.813	92.681	87.860	67.732	58.441
Services	10.453	38.677	33.459	36.279	52.555	44.531
Hotels and Restaurants	2.426	6.193	7.825	3.133	5.561	5.570
IT and BPO	2.155	14.341	8.712	15.219	12.612	11.481
Other Services	5.872	18.143	16.922	17.927	34.382	27.480
Grand Total	287.204	603.686	734.362	888.935	602.250	516.296

Source: Board of Investment, Sri Lanka.

Sri Lanka, in 1962. Also, FDI flows from India to Nepal and Sri Lanka have been noticed, with the subsidiaries focusing on exporting their products into India (Pradhan, 2008). The Indian investors have also been encouraged by the option of re-exporting to

India by benefiting from the lower tariffs on raw materials in Sri Lanka (UNCTAD, 2013). It is observed from the BOI sources that Indian investment in Sri Lanka has gone in the areas of Manufacturing (Oil, Margarine, Vanaspathi Ghee, Steel products, PVC, Furniture, Herbal, Electric items, Copper, Metals and products, Palm, Rubber, Value-Added Tea, Garments, Petroleum Products, Food processing), Housing (Residential Apartments, Building Complexes), Infrastructure (Mobile Telecommunication), Services (Computer Software), Trading Houses, etc. A number of Indian investments in the tourism sector in Sri Lanka are expected in the future (High Commission of India Colombo, 2011).

Though comparatively lower in terms of absolute value, the investment in Sri Lanka from other SAARC countries is no less important. The Maldives has invested in Sri Lanka in the area of building complex, paper products and printing, organic chemicals and value-added tea, agriculture, deep sea fishing, etc. Pakistan's investment in the country is in the areas of embroidery service, packaging, poly bags, garments, payphone network, cultivation, polythene manufacturing, call center/BPO operations, investment holding, etc. Bangladesh and Nepal have invested in trading houses and wood products, respectively.

Figure 4.9 shows the percentage distribution of various sectors in Sri Lankan FDI inflow during 2016. It is observed that the telephone and telecommunication sector tops the list with 39.74% share in aggregate FDI inflow, followed by power generation; housing and property development; and textile, wearing apparel, and leather sector with corresponding figures of 11.32%, 8.15%, and 7.27%, respectively.

4.6.4. *Trends in trade*

Sri Lanka has a fairly open and transparent trade regime, characterized by reliance on price-based measures and scant use of non-tariff measures and, in general, relatively low tariffs. Sri Lanka's main trade policy thrust continues to be aimed at achieving greater integration into the world economy. Adoption of various incentive

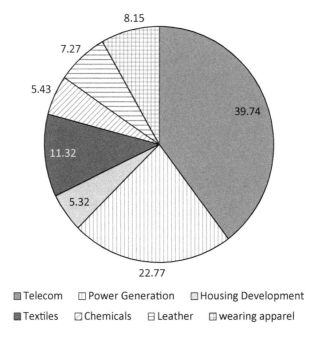

Figure 4.9:   Percentage Distribution of FDI Across the Sectors (2016) by Value of Investment

programs has resulted in a significant increase in the trade volume of Sri Lanka in recent times. Sri Lanka has also been able to diversify its trade basket and destinations to a large extent.

Table 4.15 represents the trend in Sri Lanka's trade from 2000 to 2017. Like other countries in the SAARC region, a fluctuating trend can be noticed in the total trade of Sri Lanka from 2000 to 2017. The trade value reduced to the lowest level in 2001 and reached a peak in the year 2017. Apparel and clothing accessories, tea and coffee, and rubber articles are major export items from Sri Lanka. It is noteworthy to mention that both the textile and rubber article sector are also the major recipients of FDI in Sri Lanka. Sri Lanka is also the biggest producer of tea in the world after India. In the case of import, Sri Lanka spent the maximum amount on mineral fuels and oils. This is followed by Vehicles (for example, railway wagons and tramways, etc.).

Sri Lanka has attracted FDI mainly from India, Malaysia, Hong Kong, and Japan. Telecom power generation, and manufacturing

Table 4.15: Trends of Total
Mercantile Trade in Sri Lanka
(Million USD)

Year	Trade Value (EX+IM)
2000	11,711
2001	10,789
2002	10,804
2003	11,797
2004	13,730
2005	15,180
2006	17,144
2007	19,041
2008	22,405
2009	17,394
2010	22,114
2011	30,505
2012	28,570
2013	28,211
2014	30,715
2015	29,481
2016	29,493
2017	32,189

Source: UN stat.

sectors have attracted the highest amount FDI for Sri Lanka. Major products exported by Sri Lanka are apparel and clothing accessories, tea, rubber, etc. while major import products were mineral fuels and nuclear fuels.

4.7. Conclusion

In this chapter, the trend of FDI inflows and trade in the SAARC group of countries has been presented. The chapter also described the development of FDI policy in the SAARC group of countries.

A fluctuating trend was found in case of inflow of FDI for all the selected countries. A similar result was also found in case of trade in these countries. This chapter found that all the selected countries have initiated the liberalization investment and trade policy almost during the same time period. However, even after adopting a liberalized trade and investment policy, these countries could not achieve intra-regional flow of investment at their full potential.

In Bangladesh, sectors like agro-based industry, chemicals, textiles, glass and ceramic, and food have attracted the highest amount of foreign investment. Countries like UAE, Saudi Arabia, and the United Kingdom were found to be the major investors in Bangladesh.

Bhutan is the smallest country and one of the LDCs in the SAARC region that has attracted the least amount of foreign investment. During the reference period of the research, India, Virgin Islands, and Germany were found to be the key investors in the country, while the manufacturing sector attracted the highest share of the foreign investment.

India received the highest amount of foreign investment in the SAARC region. Mauritius, Singapore, and the USA were the major investors in India. Among the SAARC countries, Sri Lanka, Nepal, and Bangladesh have also invested heavily in India.

In Nepal, agriculture and forestry, manufacturing, food, and beverage were the major recipients of foreign investment. China, USA, South Korea, and India were the major investors in Nepal. Interestingly, all the member countries of SAARC except Afghanistan and Maldives have invested in Nepal in our reference period.

Telecommunication, power generation, and textiles were the major recipient sectors of foreign investment in Sri Lanka.

In the case of most of the SAARC countries, similar products were found to be on the list of both top exports and imports. These countries have been able to diversify their trade basket as well as their trading partners. The SAARC countries were found to be importing raw products and exporting finished goods. It is observed in the chapter that all the selected SAARC member countries have benefited from the liberalization of their trade and investment regime. However, the region needs to go further to utilize its full potential. After having discussed the FDI policy, trends in FDI flows and trade, in the subsequent chapter an attempt will be made to assess the current relationship between these two variables. Since the region has experienced large inflows of FDI and at the same time seen a large expansion of international trade, there is a need to examine the relationship between these two. This is attempted empirically in Chapter 5.

References

Board of Investment (2010). Foreign Direct Investment in Bangladesh (1971–2010), Prime Minister's office, Government of Bangladesh.

Commonwealth Secretariat (2014), "Indo-Bangla Trade: Composition, Trends and the Way Forward", in Razzaque, M. and Y. Basnett (eds.), *Regional Integration in South Asia: Trends, Challenges and Prospects*. Commonwealth Secretariat, London.

DIPP. SIA New Letters, Various Issues, DIPP New Delhi.

High Commission of India Colombo (2011). India — Connects, *Economic and Business Newsletter Colombo*, 2(2).

Jigme, S. (2006). Determinants Affecting Foreign Direct Investment In Bhutan: Perception of Government Officers In "BIMSTEC" Member Countries. Department of International Business, Graduate School, the University of the Thai Chamber Of Commerce.

Kumar, N. (2003). Liberalisation, FDI Flows and Economic Development: An Indian Experience in the 1990s, *RIS-DP # 65/2003*, New Delhi, India.

Mukherjee, J., & Sinha, T. (2011). Significant Recovery, *The Hindu Survey of Indian Industry*.

Pradhan, J. P. (2008). Rise of Indian Outward FDI: What Implications does it Hold for Host Developing Countries? *Revista Economia*, 29, 9–49.

Ray, R. K. (2017). India's FDI Inflows at a Record $60.1 Billion in 2016–2017, *Hindustan Times*, New Delhi, 19 May. Retrieved from https://www.hindustantimes.com/business-news/india-s-fdi-inflows-at-a-record-60-1-billion-in-2016-17/story-7a8pt2u7e8IJttptDQcwhO.html.

Sahoo, P. (2006). Foreign Direct Investment in South Asia: Policy, Trends, Impact and Determinants, ADB Institute Discussion Paper no 56.

UNCTAD (2003). World Investment Report, UNCTAD, Geneva.

UNCTAD (2017). World Investment Report. UNCTAD , Geneva.

World Trade Organization (2004). *Trade Policy Review of Sri Lanka*, WTO, Geneva.

Chapter 5

Relationship between Trade and Investment in the SAARC Region

There exist a close relationship between trade and FDI in any economy. It has been observed that, in some cases, trade complements FDI while in some cases it is the other way round. We will investigate this important issue with regard to SAARC nations in this chapter.

5.1. Introduction

The surge in the volume of world trade and FDI in the last two decades has attracted a debate among the researchers and policymakers on the issue of the relationship between these two factors. The major questions that arise are: how they are related? If related, is the relationship supplementary or complementary to each other? That is, whether FDI enhances trade or contracts trade? Any relationship between trade and FDI can impact at least three sets of countries. First, the investing or source country, second the host or recipient country and finally a third country. From the investing country's point of view, FDI outflow may substitute trade as exports of the country will be replaced by the domestic sales in the host country by the foreign company. At the initial stage, this investment could negatively impact the investing country as the capital, production, employment generated by the investment firm will be shifted to the host country. In addition, the flight of flight will also reduce the foreign exchange earnings of the investing country, which was earlier realized through export. As against this, FDI outflow can be complementary for the investing country as it will also bring competitiveness in the foreign market and also increase export in the form of intermediate goods. In this case, the final good is produced in the host country and raw materials are supplied by the investing country. Further, the repatriation of the profit to the parent company by its subsidiary in the host country will also enhance the scope for earning foreign exchange.

From the host country's point of view, the relationship between FDI and trade can also have a similar impact. When a foreign firm starts its operation in the host country, it increases the GNP of the nation through domestic production. It procures raw materials from the domestic market and increases competitiveness. Foreign firms also create huge employment and skilled labour in the domestic market. Moreover it replaces the import of the host country, which in turn reduces its trade deficit and current account deficit. In addition to that, host countries are benefitted from the long-run spillover in the form of technology transfer, R&D, job training and advanced management skills. However, there are also possibilities of FDI crowding out domestic investment.

The nature of investment and trade also impacts the third county. If a subsidiary of the parent company is located in the third country, then it will supply intermediate goods to the host country, which in turn increases its export and finally foreign exchange earnings. In another case (in the absence of affiliate of the parent company), it may also import from the host country, which it was importing from the parent company earlier and reduce its transportation cost and finally the total import cost. This is applicable if the host country is nearer than the source country of investment. This particularly holds true in case of regional market arrangements.

Here it is to be noted that export trade like FDI is also a form of catering to the foreign market. In the initial stage generally, a firm caters to the foreign market by exporting into it and when the demand grows there, the firm finds it profitable to expand its operations in the host country instead of producing in one country and selling it in another.[1] This typically happens in the case of horizontal FDI. The major factors that play an important role in this regard are transportation cost, tariff and non-tariff barriers. The proximity-concentration hypothesis proposes that higher transaction costs resulting from various trade barriers and transportation cost encourage cross-border production expansion and thus stimulate international investment (see Krugman, 1983; Brainard, 1993). In this way, FDI substitutes exports.

But at the same time, the growing fragmentation of the production process combined with the development of distribution networks spanning across countries has led to a complementary relationship between trade and FDI. The revolution in information technology, which has opened a new medium of communication, has kickstarted a new era. This has enabled firms from less developed and transition countries to access foreign markets without making a huge investment in advertising and market research. This kind of FDI is generally referred to as vertical FDI. In this case, the source countries export the intermediate goods to the host country, which results in increasing trade between them. As the production process of the same firm or industry is spanned over more than one country, this also increases intra-industry trade.

Even though a large body of literature is available that explains the relationship between trade and FDI, they are inconclusive regarding the relationship. Some studies have reported a complementary relationship between these two, while some have advocated supplementary relationship between them (see UNCTAD, 1996; Brainard, 1997; Fontagne, 1999; Stone & Jeon, 2000; Helpman, Melitz & Yeaple, 2003; Aizenman & Noy, 2006). Further, some studies were limited to bilateral trade and FDI relationship, while others have attempted to capture the regional trade and FDI relationship (see An-loh Lin, 1995; Stone & Jeon, 2000; Graham, 1999; Brainard, 1997).

It is also pertinent to note that researchers have paid very little attention to addressing this issue with regard to the SAARC region.

---

[1] Vernon (1966) has examined this issue in terms of product life cycle theory.

It is in this context that the main objective of this chapter is to investigate the nature of the relationship between international trade and FDI in the countries in the SAARC region. The relationship will be analyzed intra-regional as well as for each of the individual countries.

5.2. Review of Literature

One of the first researches that have examined the trade and FDI linkages was conducted by Lin (1995). He explored the trade effect of the FDI for Taiwan and four ASEAN (i.e., Indonesia, Malaysia, Philippines and Thailand) countries.[2] Lin estimated the effect of Taiwan's outward FDI in a host country on export to and imports from the host country and the trade effect of inward FDI from that country. The analysis was based on time series data for the period 1972–1992. The author argued that inward FDI from all the four ASEAN countries to Taiwan was market-seeking and not export-oriented. The result finds a significant positive effect of outward FDI on export while inward FDI has no such effect on Taiwan's import from the home country.

In another work, Pfaffermayr (1996) explored the relationship between outward FDI and exports of the manufacturing sector in the Austrian economy. The analysis used time series cross-section data for seven industries in the Austrian manufacturing sector. The time period covered by the analysis was from 1981 to 1991. The results provided evidence of a significant and stable complementary relationship between FDI in the Austrian economy. The causal relationships between the indicators at both directions were also established in the analysis. The author argued that R&D intensity affects both FDI and exports positively. The author also argued that labour intensity determines FDI positively, whereas exports depend positively on capital intensity.

Stone and Jeon (2000) analyzed the relationship between FDI and trade in the Asia-Pacific region during the time period starting from 1970 to 1994. They used gravity model analysis for the

---

[2] ASEAN countries consist of Indonesia, Malaysia, Philippines, Thailand, Cambodia, Singapore, Laos, Vietnam, Brunei and Myanmar.

estimation of the result. They found a positive and complementary relationship between trade and FDI. The authors argued that FDI enhances bilateral trade flows. The results established that higher income countries are more prone to specialize in trade compared to lower per capita income countries.

Clausing (2000) examined the relationship between trade and FDI for US MNEs. The research was based on two groups of panel data for the period 1977–1994. The first data set covered information about the operations of American MNEs in 29 different host countries and data about American exports to them. The main aim of this data set was to find out the relationship between FDI and export. The second data set replaced the export by the import of the first data set with the aim to analyze the import and FDI relation. Clausing reported that FDI positively influences trade. A robust complementary relation also exists between intra-firm trade and FDI and a weaker complementary relationship exists between inter-firm trade and FDI.

Marchant, Cornell and Koo (2002) explored the trade and investment relationship in the case of US processed food exports to East Asian countries. The analysis used data from 1989 to 1998 and followed SIC code 20. The results showed a bidirectional complementary relationship between FDI inflows and exports from the United States to the East Asian countries. The estimation of the results led to the conclusion that interest rates were negatively influenced by US FDI inflows in East Asian countries.

Chaisrisawatsuk and Chaisrisawatsuk (2007) investigated the bi-directional effects of international trade and investment. The analysis covered 29 OECD countries and six ASEAN nations. The time period considered in the research was from 1980 to 2004. The analysis also employed gravity model approach to investigate the relationship between international trade and foreign investment. The authors argued that greater the international trade between countries, the higher level of FDI it generates and vice versa. The estimation results implied that a one percentage increase in trade can lead to a 1.21% increase in FDI inflows. The authors argued since trade liberalization is welfare improving, FDI induced by trade expansion would also improve social welfare.

Hailu (2010) analyzed the relationship between FDI and trade balance of 16 African countries. The time period covered in the research was from 1980 to 2007. The analysis applied random effect technique and the least square dummy variable (LSDV) regression method on the panel form of data for the analysis. The author concluded that MNEs in Sub-Saharan Africa are not just export-oriented but also import-dependent. The results established a positive relation for both export and import with FDI in the African region.

The research studies discussed thus far have established a close positive link between international trade and investment. As opposed to this, other studies have concluded that FDI and trade are the substitute for one another.

Gopinath, Pick and Vasavada (1997) explored the trade and FDI relationship for 10 developed countries with the time period covering 1982–1994. The results found a supplementary relationship between foreign sale and FDI. The results found most of the FDI is tariff jumping in nature.

In a similar work, Belderbos and Sleuwaegen (1998) also found that Japanese FDI in European countries was tariff jumping in nature and thus substitutes export. The analysis covered the electronic industry of Japan for the time period from 1980 to 1995.

The National Board of Trade (2008) conducted firm-level analysis for the Swedish multinational firms and their trade and FDI activities. The reference period for the research was from 1980 to 2005. The analysis used a three-country model of FDI with heterogeneous firms, built on Norbäck, Urban and Westerberg (2007). The results showed that with the growing world economy, both the Swedish exports as well as the FDI have increased. The research found that world income growth promote a platform for FDI, in terms of affiliate exports to third countries, more than the Swedish firm exports, in relative terms. That is, as the world economy grows, firms may opt to supply foreign markets through FDI instead of exports — in relative terms and thus it substitute the trade.

Some researchers have also found both the relationships at the same time. For instance, Connor and Salin (1997) examined trade and FDI behavior of food processing firms in the United States. The research covered five major firms in the food processing industry. The time period covered by the analysis was from 1978 to 1993. The paper categorized the export and FDI of these firms into three distinct phases. In the first phase, the firms cater to overseas market by export. In the second phase, they adopt FDI but at a relatively low level. In the final stage, the firms adopt a substitution strategy at a higher level of FDI. In other words, more intense FDI activities are undertaken. The results found both complementary and supplementary relationship between trade and FDI.

Similarly, Amiti, David and Katharine (2000) examined the trade and FDI relationship in the United States with its 25 major trading partners. The research was conducted covering the time period of 1983–1994. The results established both complementary and supplementary relationship between trade and FDI. The results indicate that horizontal FDI is more likely to dominate when two countries are similar in terms of relative skill endowments and size, and trade costs between them are moderate to high and hence FDI and trade are substitutes. Whereas vertical FDI is likely to dominate when countries differ in terms of relative skill endowments and size, and trade costs are low, FDI and trade become complementary to each other. Thus, it is clear from the works reviewed above that the relationship between trade and FDI are inconclusive. Further, very few studies have been conducted for the SAARC countries as a whole or even for any member country. It is this lacuna the current chapter is has attempted to bridge. In the next section, the trade and investment flow in the SAARC region are presented.

5.3. Trade and Investment Flows in the SAARC Region

South Asian countries have been immensely benefitted from their trade and investment policy liberalization process. The vast and advanced global production network of the MNCs investing in the region has helped them to expand their exports. Foreign affiliates establishing export-oriented production bases in the region have also helped them to earn huge amount of foreign exchange. The garment sector in Bangladesh, rubber goods in Sri Lanka and the automobile sector in India have attracted a huge amount of FDI in this regard. However, bulk FDI inflow in the region has been market-seeking due to its large consumer base. Another main objective of the foreign investors in the region was to tap the abundant amount of natural resources and skilled labor at low wages. The domestic production of the MNCs has also helped the region to curb its import to a large extent. The value of both trade and investment has increased in the region during the last few years. This is evident in Table 5.1.

Table 5.1 reveals both trade and FDI have increased tremendously during the 2000–2016 period in the South Asian region. The

Table 5.1:   Trade and Investment in SAARC Region (in US$)

Year	FDI Inflow	Trade (X+M)
2000	4.7	145
2001	6.3	144
2002	7.1	158
2003	5.5	191
2004	7.8	248
2005	11.3	330
2006	26.3	400
2007	32.6	490
2008	54.6	651
2009	39.5	537
2010	31.3	719
2011	40.0	945
2012	27.7	963
2013	32.6	964
2014	39.3	981
2015	48.8	850
2016	50.4	822

Source: Authors calculation based on UNCTAD data.

data reveals a constant growth in both the indicators up to 2008 while a fluctuating trend was noticed in the following period. The amount of the FDI inflows was very low as compared to the total trade value. However, the value of the FDI inflows, which was only $4.7 billion in 2000, has increased to more than $50 billion in 2016. It is important to note that the highest amount of foreign investment inflow in the region was in 2008. But after that, a fluctuating trend was noticed in this regard as noted earlier. The global economic meltdown was one of the main reasons behind it, and it was reflected not only in the South Asian economy but also on other regions.

The intraregional flows of FDI are very limited in the SAARC region. Different policy measures have taken place to encourage trade and investment in the region. Creation of the SAARC Preferential Trading Arrangement (SAPTA) and then superseding it by the South Asian Free Trade Area (SAFTA) is a major step in this process. But it has made a very little impact on the performance of the trade and investment flows. From the available data, India emerges as the major investing country in the region. It is the only country in the region which has invested in all other countries in the region. Tables 5.2 and 5.3 show the intraregional FDI flows in South Asia.

Table 5.2 reflects the intraregional FDI inflows in SAARC countries, while Table 5.3 displays India's investment in other countries in the region. The data for outward FDI from Maldives, Pakistan and Bhutan were not available so we had to restrict our analysis to the remaining countries only. As the available data were not in common currency units we were unable to compare them. Moreover, the availability of the data restricted the analysis up-to a much older period.

Table 5.2 suggests that intra-regional FDI inflows with SAARC countries haven't witnessed any significant movement or rise. Major economies like India, Sri Lanka and Nepal have received some amount of inflows though in absolute value they are quite meager. India has received a substantial amount of investment from Sri Lanka and Bhutan during 2007–2008. Nepal received a maximum amount of 2341 million Nepali rupees of inflows during

Table 5.2:   Intra-regional FDI Inflows in SAARC Countries (Excludes India)

	India					Bangladesh		Nepal				Sri Lanka	
	2007–08	2009–10	2010–11	2011–12	2012–13	2006	2010	2008–09	2009–10	2010–11	2011–12	2009	2010
India	0	0	0	0	0	5.78	5.38	2341.3	3993.5	7007.2	2298	77.7	110.2
Bangladesh		0	0	0	0.03	0	0	28.5	100	9.80	12.6	0	0
Nepal	21.07		0	0.01	0	0	0			—	—	0	0.1
Sri Lanka	132.92	59.73	3.89	6.4	6.59	0	0.16			10.0	4	0	0
Maldives	4.11	17.16				2.0	0			0	0	0.3	1.4
Pakistan			0	0	0			2.4	0	0	7.33	0	0
Bhutan	137.03	0	0			0	0			0	0	0	0
Total World inflows to Individual country	24575	19427	3120.6	35120.8	22423.5	1118	35.96	5355.5	9100	10050.7	7140.8	402	383.4

Note: Nepal data are in million Nepali rupees other figures are in million US dollars.

Sources: Authors' calculation based on data collected from Board of Investment (BOI): Bangladesh, Sri Lanka, Pakistan, SIA: India; Department of Industries (DOI) Nepal.

Table 5.3: Indian Investment in SAARC Countries (Million US$)

	2007–08	2009–10	2010–11	2011–12	2012–13	2006	2014–15	2015–16	2016–17
Bangladesh		0	0		0.03	0	8.4	8.8	29.6
Nepal		21.07	0	0.01	0	0	5.4	1.7	21.9
Sri Lanka	132.92	59.73	3.89	6.4	6.59	0	89.0	57.8	131.4
Maldives	4.11	17.16	0			0	13.01	2.8	6.9
Pakistan		0	0		0	0	0	0	0
Bhutan	137.03	0	0		0	0	0.188	0.12	0.4
Total World inflows to Individual country	24575	19427	3120.6	35120.8	22423.5	1118			

Source: Reserve Bank of India.

2008–2009, which further increased to Nepali Rs. 3993 million during 2009–2010 and subsequently in 2010–2011. FDI inflows into Nepal were predominantly driven by Indian investments. Sri Lanka also received FDI inflows from India during this period, which was to the tune of $78 million. Bangladesh has also invested in Nepal during 2009–2010 to the tune of $100 million. Among the SAARC countries, India has received maximum FDI inflows from the world during 2007–2008 which declined during 2009–2010 to $19,427 million from $24,575 during 2007–2008.

During the last four to five years, Nepal, Sri Lanka and Bangladesh have received the maximum FDI inflows from SAARC countries. Nepal has registered around 44% of India's investment and about 45% of South Asian share during 2008–2009 and 2009–2010. Similarly, Sri Lanka has increased its South Asian share from 19.4% to 29.13% from 2009 to 2010. Indian investment in Sri Lanka witnessed a big surge during 2016–2017. The investment mainly flowed to the wholesale trading sector. Bangladesh has witnessed a dramatic increase in its South Asian share from 0.70% in 2006 to 15.41% in 2010. Whereas India as a major investor in the region has occupied a much smaller share of 1.12% in 2007–2008, which has further declined to 0.5 in 2009–2010. Being an important economy, its share has fallen so dramatically, which possibly could be because India has invested elsewhere during this period than South Asia.

It is a well-established fact that trade and FDI are closely related. Evidence suggests the existence of a two-way relationship between these variables. The same is true for SAARC nations as well. Before investigating the type of direction of the relationship between these two variables in the South Asian context, one needs to understand the flow of intra-regional trade in SAARC. In this context, Table 5.4 displays the intra-regional trade among SAARC countries.

Even after the creation of SAPTA in 1995 and superseding it by SAFTA in 2006, the intraregional trade flow among the South Asian countries are still very low or negligible. As per estimation, only 4% of the total trade of South Asia is directed toward the region (Moazzem, 2013). This may be because of the disparities in the market size and different consumption patterns among the countries. The similarities in the goods produced in the region also may be a reason behind it. For example, both India and Bangladesh are major producers of rice and both India and Sri Lanka are major producers of tea. India, Sri Lanka, Bangladesh and Pakistan all produce a substantial amount of garments. However, the total production process is fragmented among these countries. Thus, we cannot expect them to go

Table 5.4:   Intraregional Trade among SAARC Countries in 2016 (Billion US$)

	India	Nepal	Pakistan	Sri Lanka	Bangladesh
India		6.21	1.98	4.38	6.40
Bhutan	0.502	0.01	0.00	0.00	0.04
Maldives	0.19	0.00	0.01	0.18	0.01
Nepal	4.91	NA	0.00	0.00	0.00
Pakistan	2.05	0.00	NA	0.37	0.83
Sri Lanka	4.75	0.00	0.31	NA	0.14
Bangladesh	6.346	0.06	0.70	0.14	NA

Note: Data for Bangladesh is for 2015.
Source: Authors calculation based on UN COMTRADE (WITS) data.

beyond a certain potential and create higher intra-regional trade. The trade pattern among the SAARC nations is also much skewed. For instance, Nepal and Sri Lanka imported around 46% and 16% of their imports from India, respectively, in the year 2010 (Jain & Singh, 2009). A huge amount of informal trade among the member countries is a major hindrance to increasing intraregional trade in the region. According to Chaudhari (1995), India's total informal exports and imports in 1992–1993 were about $299 million and $14 million, respectively. In the same year, official exports and imports were about $349 million and $8 million, respectively. The total value of the unrecorded import from India by Bangladesh in 2002–2003, estimated by the World Bank, was more than $500 million. This was around 42% of Bangladesh's recorded imports from India, or about 30% of total imports (recorded plus smuggled) in the same year (World Bank, 2006). Paper products, sanitaryware and rice are some the major imported (illegally) goods from India.

As per Khan *et al.* (2007), the total value of the informal trade between India and Pakistan in 2005 was around $545 million, out of which Pakistan's imports from India was estimated to be around $535 million and exports to India $10.4 million (Khan *et al.*, 2007). Cloth, tires, pharmaceuticals, textile machinery, cosmetics and livestock are majorly traded goods between these two countries. The political difference between India and Pakistan also poses a major threat in encouraging trade in the region. In the case of Nepal, the amount of India's informal trade was around 10 times of the legal trade (see Muni, 1992).

The data shown in Table 5.4 reveals that India is the biggest trading country in the region followed by Pakistan. Among all the countries in the region, India's biggest trading partner is Bangladesh transacting more than $6.3 billion in trade in 2016, while Nepal is second with $4.9 billion in the same year. The least amount of trade value in case of India was captured for Maldives and Bhutan. Interestingly, the same is also true for all other SAARC member countries except Pakistan.

Having discussed intra-regional trade and investment flows among SAARC group of countries, in the next section, the sources of data and the methodology used to examine the relationship is elaborated upon.

5.4. The Econometric Methodology

5.4.1. *Data sources*

We have used various sources for the collection of the data. We tapped both country-specific and international sources for the data collection. The details of the sources for different variables for different countries are as follows.

In the case of Bangladesh, FDI inflow data was collected from the Board of Investment publication *Foreign Direct Investment in Bangladesh (1971–2010)* up to 2010. And for 2011 and 2012, data was extracted from another research publication "Fluctuation of FDI Inflow in Bangladesh — Obstacles and Potentials: An Issue of Policy Failure." Beyond 2012 data were received from the Board of Investment officials with a special request. We use the online website of State Bank of Pakistan (the country's central bank) for the collection of FDI inflow data for Pakistan. The Board of Investment, Sri Lanka, provided the same data in case of Sri Lanka. We also use the annual reports of the Sri Lankan Central Bank. Secretariat for Industrial Assistance (SIA), newsletters of the Department of Industrial Policy and Promotion, Ministry of Commerce, Government of India, was referred for the collection of FDI inflow data in case of India. Various issues of *Industrial Statistics* published by the Department of Industry, Government of Nepal, were referred for collecting data on FDI inflows in Nepal. The UNCTAD publication on foreign direct investment in LDCs was also used for filling up the missing data in case of Nepal.

GDP and exchange rate data for all the selected countries were extracted from the UN statistics website. For border and language data, the websites of the concerned countries were used. The data on distance was collected from Macalester college website. Export and import data for all the selected countries were collected from UN COMTRADE, accessed from the World Integrated Trade Solution (WITS) online database.

5.4.2. *The model*

As mentioned earlier in the chapter, the objective of the chapter is to estimate the relationship between FDI and trade in SAARC countries. In order to estimate the relationship, the gravity model has been applied. It was Carey in 1860, who first used Newton's law of universal gravitation in the field of social sciences. Subsequently, the gravity equation or model got wide acceptance in the social and behavior sciences research. The model envisages that trade between the two nations depends positively on the size of their economies while negatively on their distance. The size of the economy is measured in terms of GDP and population of the trading nations. The distinctive feature of the gravity model is its distance variable, which measures geographical or cultural proximity between the two trading nations. The other distinctive parameters of the model are dummy variables, such as common official language, border, common colonial ties, country's sea access, etc.

Following Carey, a wide range of research studies were conducted in the area of international trade. Tinbergen (1962) used a simple form of the gravity model of bilateral trade in estimating bilateral trade flows. The gravity model has also been applied to flows of people and capital (direct and indirect). Anderson (1979) explored the gravity equation model assuming product differentiation. Bergstrand (1985) analyzed the theoretical determination of bilateral trade association in gravity equations with simple monopolistic competition models. In the last two decades, the model has also been used to analyze various aspects of FDI (Brainard, 1997; Deardorff 1997, Braconier, Norbäck & Urban, 2005; Bergstrand, Egger & Larch, 2008).

In our analysis, we have used panel data of SAARC countries during 2000–2016. The panel data generally addresses the presence of heterogeneity in individual firms, sectors or countries. The panel data detect and measure effects that may not be observed in time series or cross-section data. The panel data can be analyzed using two regression technique, i.e., fixed effect model and random effect model. In the fixed effect estimation, we assume that the individual specific effect is correlated with the independent variables while in the random effect estimator, the individual specific effects are uncorrelated with the independent variables. In the current analysis, we apply both fixed and random effect estimator. However, we find that in our method of inquiry, the appropriate technique would be a random effect model. The random effect model allows us to estimate the shrunken residuals and provides us the possibility of accounting for differential effectiveness through the use of random coefficients models.

In the empirical estimation, two distinct modified gravity equations for the export and import variable is used. We have developed a two-way model in order to capture the time period and specific country effect. Three countries — Bhutan, Afghanistan and the Maldives — have not been considered for analysis due to lack of data. The analysis is carried out for the top five investing and trading partners of the selected SAARC countries.

The modified gravity equation for SAARC countries is given in equation (1). The model explicitly incorporates the determinant of trade (exports/imports) by FDI and other characteristics such as GDP, exchange rate, border and distance factors.

$$EX_{it} = \beta_0 + \beta_1 FDI_{it} + \beta_2 GDP_{it} + \beta_3 ER_{it} + \beta_4 Border_{it} + \beta_5 dist_{it} + \mu_i + \varepsilon_{it}, \tag{5.1}$$

$$IM_{it} = \beta_0 + \beta_1 FDI_{it} + \beta_2 GDP_{it} + \beta_3 ER_{it} + \beta_4 Border_{it} + \beta_5 dist_{it} + \mu_i + \varepsilon_{it}, \tag{5.2}$$

Here, t is the time period from $1,\ldots, T$ (i.e., 2000–2016), i is the countries from $I,\ldots, N$, EX_i is the export of the country i to SAARC member countries, IM_i is the import of the country i from SAARC member countries, FDI_i is the FDI inflow from the country i to SAARC member countries, GDP_i is the GDP of country i, ER_i is the exchange rate of country i, $Border_i$ is the dummy variable for the common border between country i and SAARC member countries, $dist_i$ is the distance between country i and SAARC member countries, μ_i is the unobservable individual effects, ε_{it} is the error term.

The current chapter assumes that the export and import of the SAARC member countries as dependent variables. FDI inflows from selected countries, GDP and exchange rate of the investing countries are chosen as the independent variables. The common border with investing countries and a common language with investing countries are also considered as an independent dummy variable in the model. The variables that are expected to determine FDI flows are carefully chosen based on previous literature and the availability of dataset for the selected period. The model converted the values of all the variables into a log, with the exception of distance, exchange rate and dummy variables. The details regarding the data sources and the construction of variables are explained briefly in the following section.

5.4.3. *Variable construction approach*

The present chapter conducted a rigorous exercise to select the top investing countries in the SAARC region. First, we collected data on FDI inflows in all the SAARC countries from different source countries for the period 2000–2016. Then we calculated the average of the inflows for each member countries from various source countries. Finally, the average values were sorted in a descending order and top five investing countries were selected for each of the SAARC member nations for further analysis. Here it is to be noted that the share of these top five countries in the total investment of the host country was more than 70% in all the cases. However, due to lack of availability of the proper data (continuous and source country-wise), the chapter dropped three countries of the SAARC region.

In case of dependent variable data were not directly available on COMTRADE, i.e., reporter countries had not reported export figures (FOB), so we had to rely on the import figures (CIF) of the partner countries. The CIF values were adjusted into FOB values by subtracting 10%, as the standard difference between FOB and CIF are 10%. The harmonized system (HS) nomenclature of 1996 was used for the trade data. The exercise was carried out in case of

Bangladesh's export figures from 2007 to 2015 and for Pakistan's and Sri Lanka's export, it was for 2009 and 2016. For Nepal's export, it was for 2008 and 2016.

The FDI inflow data for all countries were available in US dollar terms except for Nepal. Thus, the data of Nepal was converted into US dollars using the Nepalese exchange rate with US dollar for the relevant year. The FDI data of Bangladesh was divided into joint venture and 100% equity. Therefore, to obtain the total FDI flows to Bangladesh, these two sources were added. We assume the value one (1) for positive common border and common language and zero (0) for negative common border and common language.

5.4.4. *Estimation results*

Bangladesh Exports

Dependent Variable: LNEX

Method: Panel Least Squares

Sample: 2000–2016

Periods included: 17

Cross-sections included: 5

Total panel (balanced) observations: 85

Variable	Coefficient	Std. Error	*t*-Statistic	Prob.
LNDST	1.281481	0.291898	4.390168	0.0000
ER	−2.225792	1.108646	−2.007667	0.0493
LNFDI	0.206689	0.072308	2.858476	0.0059
LNGDP	0.864410	0.134087	6.446632	0.0000
BORDER	1.952081	0.366079	5.332405	0.0000
C	−16.49260	2.468804	−6.680400	0.0000

(Continued)

(*Continued*)

R^2	0.834488 Mean dependent var	5.757428
Adjusted R^2	0.820461 S.D. dependent var	1.766142
S.E. of regression	0.748350 Akaike info criterion	2.345873
Sum squared resid	33.04162 Schwarz criterion	2.546586
Log-likelihood	−70.24088 Hannan–Quinn criteria	2.425067
F statistic	59.49385 Durbin–Watson stat	0.698338
Prob(F statistic)	0.000000	

The empirical results obtained from panel OLS regression pertaining to the export of Bangladesh explain 83% (R^2) variation in the model. Thus, the explanatory variables included in the equation explain 83% of the variation in the dependent variable. The F statistics is 59.49, and the probability of F statistics is 0.0000, which shows that the results are statistically significant and the null hypothesis of the independent variables having no effect on export is rejected. The results explain that distance, FDI, GDP, exchange rate and border are statistically significant and have expected sign except for distance. Distance is positively related to export in Bangladesh. This means greater the distance, higher was the export from Bangladesh. From this, it may be concluded that in the case of Bangladesh, the proposition of the gravity model that closer the countries higher is the trade between them does not apply. It is possible that the distance and export are directly related because 80% of Bangladesh export consists of garments and a large part of these exports go to the United States and the European Union. For instance, in the year 2009–2010, Bangladesh exported $4888 million of garments to these two destinations, which were 30% of their total export. As expected, the exchange rate is negatively related to export. GDP is positively related to export, which means higher production of goods and services increases the export from Bangladesh. The border is positively related to Bangladesh exports. The total export of Bangladesh to SAARC countries was $421 million, of which almost 72% was to India. The possible reason for this may be the cultural similarities, same consumption pattern and common language.

Bangladesh's Imports

Dependent Variable: LNIM

Method: Panel Least Squares

Sample: 2000–2016

Periods included: 17

Cross-sections included: 5

Total panel (balanced) observations: 85

Variable	Coefficient	Std. Error	t-Statistic	Prob.
LNDST	−2.504300	0.156350	−16.01730	0.0000
ER	−0.227773	0.593826	−0.383569	0.7027
LNFDI	0.048163	0.038730	1.243541	0.2186
LNGDP	1.027812	0.071821	14.31069	0.0000
BORDER	−1.260736	0.196083	−6.429589	0.0000
C	12.90485	1.322370	9.758881	0.0000

R^2	0.890719 Mean dependent var	6.595698
Adjusted R^2	0.881458 S.D. dependent var	1.164217
S.E. of regression	0.400840 Akaike info criterion	1.097256
Sum squared resid	9.479679 Schwarz criterion	1.297968
Log-likelihood	−29.66081 Hannan–Quinn criteria	1.176450
F statistic	96.17824 Durbin–Watson stat	0.680249
Prob(F statistic)	0.000000	

The result also shows that FDI has positively impacted the export from Bangladesh. Relating the theory of investment with the above results, it can be concluded that most of the FDI flows into the Bangladesh economy were vertical in nature. The theory of investment suggests that vertical FDI leads to higher export if the raw material is produced in the host country. Against this, if finished goods are produced in the host country then the import of the host country increases. In either case, vertical FDI leads to enhancement in the total trade. Being a small and less developed economy, Bangladesh has been able to attract a more vertical form of FDI than horizontal. And a higher amount of vertical FDI has thus complemented exports from Bangladesh.

The empirical results obtained from panel OLS regression for import of Bangladesh shows that regression explains 89% (R^2) variation in the model. Thus, the explanatory variables included in the equation explain 89% of the variation in the dependent variable. The F statistics is 96.17, and the probability of F statistics is 0.0000, which shows that the results are statistically significant and the null hypothesis of the independent variables having no effect on import is rejected. The results explain that distance, GDP, FDI and exchange rate are statistically significant and has expected sign except for border. Distance is negatively related to import from Bangladesh, which means that greater distance decreases import from Bangladesh. GDP is positively related to import, which means higher production of goods and services increases import from Bangladesh. FDI is positively related, which means it has increased import of Bangladesh. Exchange rate is negatively related to import, which means a higher exchange rate decreases import from Bangladesh. In the case of Bangladesh, FDI has been attracted mostly by industries that cater to foreign market, e.g., garment industry. In 2012, around 70% of the raw materials used in this sector were imported. This sector gets most of its raw materials from foreign countries. The border is negatively related in case of import from Bangladesh. Bangladesh has imported more from distant countries than the neighboring ones like India or China. In 2012, the United States and the European Union were the top importing partners of Bangladesh.

India's Exports

Dependent Variable: LNEX

Method: Panel Least Squares

Sample: 2000–2016

Periods included: 17

Cross-sections included: 5

Total panel (balanced) observations: 85

Variable	Coefficient	Std. Error	*t*-Statistic	Prob.
LNDST	0.689372	0.293943	2.345260	0.0223
ER	0.452450	0.676974	0.668341	0.5065
LNFDI	0.210272	0.044094	4.768746	0.0000
LNGDP	0.448878	0.036418	12.32575	0.0000
BORDER	−2.345260	0.452031	−14.09764	0.0000
C	−6.194002	2.167493	−2.857681	0.0059

R^2	0.862984 Mean dependent var	7.934712
Adjusted R^2	0.853850 S.D. dependent var	1.387977
S.E. of regression	0.530618 Akaike info criterion	1.644255
Sum squared resid	16.89334 Schwarz criterion	1.811516
Log-likelihood	−48.43830 Hannan–Quinn criteria	1.710250
F statistic	94.47636 Durbin–Watson stat	0.456411
Prob(*F* statistic)	0.000000	

The regression model for export of India explains 86% varia-tion. The results of the regression indicate that dependent variables included in the model explain 86% of the variation in the dependent variable. The *F* statistics is 94.47, and the probability of *F* statistics is 0.0000, which shows that the results are statistically significant and the null hypothesis of the independent variables having no effect on export is rejected. The results explain that distance, GDP, FDI and border are statistically significant and have expected sign except for border, distance and exchange rate. Distance is negatively related to export from India, which means greater the distance higher the export from India. Here, the results show a positive relationship between export and distance, i.e., greater the distance higher is the trade. Most of the FDI inflows in India were from distant countries like the United States, UK and the Netherlands. The countries like the United States, UAE and UK were also the major trading partners of India in 2012. GDP is positively related to export, which means higher production of goods and services increases export from India. FDI is positively related, which confirms that higher inflow of FDI has helped India to increase its export. The common border or nearer destinations have not played an important role in India's trade and FDI. Exchange rate is positively related to export, which means higher exchange rate increases export from India. It is possible that most of the export items of India are not sensitive to the fluctuation in the exchange rate.

Thus, from the above discussion, it can be asserted that in the case of India the gravity model is not applicable. The complementary relationship was also found between export and FDI.

India's Imports

Dependent Variable: LNIM
Method: Panel Least Squares
Sample: 2000–2016
Periods included: 17
Cross-sections included: 5
Total panel (balanced) observations: 85

Variable	Coefficient	Std. Error	t-Statistic	Prob.
LNDST	−2.558226	0.463660	−5.517457	0.0000
ER	−0.002250	1.067847	−0.002107	0.9983
LNFDI	0.107996	0.069553	1.552723	0.1257
LNGDP	1.073574	0.057445	18.68871	0.0000
BORDER	1.794710	2.560345	0.069553	0.3214
C	14.26942	3.418967	4.173606	0.0001

(Continued)

(Continued)

R^2	0.901770 Mean dependent var	7.272004
Adjusted R^2	0.895221 S.D. dependent var	2.585724
S.E. of regression	0.836988 Akaike info criterion	2.555791
Sum squared resid	42.03298 Schwarz criterion	2.723051
Log-likelihood	−78.06319 Hannan–Quinn criteria	2.621786
F statistic	137.7023 Durbin–Watson stat	0.186372
Prob (F statistic)	0.000000	7.272004

The empirical results obtained from panel OLS regression in case of import from India shows that regression explains 90% (R^2) variation in the model. Thus, the explanatory variables included in the equation explain 90% of the variation in the dependent variable. The F statistics is 137.70 and the probability of F statistics is 0.0000, which shows that the results are statistically significant and the null hypothesis of the independent variables having no effect on import is rejected. The results explain that distance, border, GDP and FDI are statistically significant and have the expected sign. Distance is positively related to import from India, which means greater distance reduces import from India. Here the proposition of the gravity model was verified. GDP is positively related to import, which means higher production of goods and services increases imports from India. The relationship between import and FDI in India was found to be complementary. Exchange rate is negatively related to import, which means a higher exchange rate decreases import from India.

Nepal's Exports

Dependent Variable: LNEX

Method: Panel Least Squares

Sample: 2000–2016

Periods included: 17

Cross-sections included: 6

Total panel (balanced) observations: 102

(Continued)

(*Continued*)

Variable	Coefficient	Std. Error	*t*-Statistic	Prob.
LNDST	−5.456379	0.476670	−11.44687	0.0000
ER	−2.534529	1.084854	2.336285	0.0223
LNFDI	0.655084	0.173650	3.772436	0.0003
LNGDP	2.775933	0.226683	12.24587	0.0000
BORDER	−5.549051	0.608340	−9.121626	0.0000
C	8.465617	1.900856	4.453582	0.0000

R^2	0.788584	Mean dependent var	2.931906
Adjusted R^2	0.773903	S.D. dependent var	2.141235
S.E. of regression	1.018150	Akaike info criterion	2.947656
Sum squared resid	74.63736	Schwarz criterion	3.128941
Log-likelihood	−108.9586	Hannan–Quinn criteria	3.020227
F statistic	53.71229	Durbin–Watson stat	0.772838
Prob(F statistic)	0.000000		

The result of the estimation for export of Nepal shows a 78% variation in the model. This means that the independent variables included in the model explain 78% of the variation in the dependent variable. Here, the *F* statistics is found to be 53.71, and the probability of *F* statistics is 0.0000, which shows that the results are statistically significant and the null hypothesis of the independent variables having no effect on export is rejected. The results explain that distance, exchange rate, GDP and border are statistically significant and has the expected sign except for border. Distance is negatively related to export from Nepal, which means greater distance reduces export from Nepal. The results for Nepal has also been verified with the assumptions of the gravity model. Most of the exporting goods of Nepal like handicrafts, processed foods are in demand in countries like UAE and Japan. The exchange rate is negatively related to export, which means higher exchange rate decreases export from Nepal. GDP is positively related to export, which means higher production of goods and services increases export from Nepal.

The relationship between export and FDI in Nepal was found to be complementary. Following the theory, it can be mentioned that being a less developed and very small economy in size, Nepal has attracted more vertical FDI, which has complemented the export from Nepal.

Nepal's Imports

Dependent Variable: LNIM

Method: Panel Least Squares

Sample: 2000–2016

Periods included: 17

Cross-sections included: 6

Total panel (balanced) observations: 102

Variable	Coefficient	Std. Error	t-Statistic	Prob.
LNDST	–1.927284	0.551723	–3.493210	0.0008
ER	4.349847	1.255667	3.464172	0.0009
LNFDI	0.247940	0.200992	1.233582	0.2214
LNGDP	1.180286	0.262375	4.498470	0.0000
BORDER	1.499551	0.704125	2.129667	0.0366
C	–1.559179	2.200150	–0.708669	0.4808

R^2	0.801208 Mean dependent var	3.804187
Adjusted R^2	0.787403 S.D. dependent var	2.555859
S.E. of regression	1.178460 Akaike info criterion	3.240098
Sum squared resid	99.99135 Schwarz criterion	3.421383
Log-likelihood	–120.3638 Hannan–Quinn criteria	3.312670
F statistic	58.03768 Durbin–Watson stat	0.872582
Prob (F statistic)	0.000000	

The empirical results in case of import from Nepal show 80% variation in the model. This result indicates that the explanatory variables included in the equation explain 80% of the variation in the dependent variable. The *F* statistics is 58.03 and the probability of *F* statistics is 0.0000, which shows that the results are statistically significant and the null hypothesis of the independent variables having no effect on import is rejected. The results explain that distance and GDP are statistically significant and have the expected sign except for exchange rate. Distance is negatively related to import from Nepal, which means greater distance reduces import from Nepal. GDP is positively related to import, which means higher production of goods and services increases imports from Nepal. A closer border increases import from Nepal. Exchange rate is positively related to import, which means higher exchange rate increases import to Nepal. This reflects that Nepal imports those goods that are less sensitive to changes in the exchange rate.

Similar to export, import from Nepal is also found to be in accordance with the assumptions of the gravity model. Nepal has received more FDI from the nearer destinations. A higher level of vertical FDI inflows in Nepal has complemented import from Nepal. Various incentives given to the export-oriented FDI in the form of tax holidays and subsidized land have also played a positive role in attracting vertical FDI in Nepal.

Pakistan's Exports

Dependent Variable: LNEX

Method: Panel Least Squares

Sample: 2000–2016

Periods included: 17

Cross-sections included: 6

Total panel (balanced) observations: 102

Variable	Coefficient	Std. Error	*t*-Statistic	Prob.
LNDST	0.566930	0.241537	2.347178	0.0216
ER	−1.540020	0.826482	1.863345	0.0664

(Continued)

(*Continued*)

LNFDI	0.170207	0.040322	4.221225	0.0001
LNGDP	0.366001	0.042935	8.524527	0.0000
BORDER	−1.560971	0.131533	1.863345	0.0000
C	−6.189967	1.785131	−3.467514	0.0009

R^2	0.809928	Mean dependent var	5.521636
Adjusted R^2	0.799513	S.D. dependent var	1.620280
S.E. of regression	0.725493	Akaike info criterion	2.258024
Sum squared resid	38.42278	Schwarz criterion	2.409095
Log-likelihood	−83.06294	Hannan–Quinn criteria	2.318501
F statistic	77.76625	Durbin–Watson stat	0.306052
Prob(F statistic)	0.000000		

The result of the estimation for export of Pakistan shows 80% variation in the model. This means that the independent variables included in the model explain 80% of the variation in the dependent variable. Here, the F statistics found 77.77, and the probability of F statistics is 0.0000, which shows that the results are statistically significant and the null hypothesis of the independent variables having no effect on export is rejected. The results explain that distance, exchange rate, GDP and border are statistically significant. All the variables have shown unexpected signs except GDP and FDI. Distance is positively related to export from Pakistan, which means greater distance increases export from Pakistan. Here it is opposed to the assumption of the gravity model. As the export basket of Pakistan is similar to the other neighboring countries in the region, it has to find a market for its products in the distant locations. For example, India and Bangladesh both produce a huge amount of garments to supply in the foreign market. Exchange rate is positively related to export, which means higher exchange rate increases export from Pakistan. This suggests that exporting items of Pakistan are not very sensitive to the changes in the exchange rate. The major exports of Pakistan are raw cotton, yarn and garments. GDP is positively related to export, which means higher production of goods and services increases export from Pakistan. The positive sign of FDI has confirmed the complementary relationship between export and FDI. Higher FDI inflow has enabled Pakistan to export more.

Pakistan's Imports

Dependent Variable: LNIM

Method: Panel Least Squares

Sample: 2000–2016

Periods included: 17

Cross-sections included: 6

Total panel (balanced) observations: 102

Variable	Coefficient	Std. Error	t-Statistic	Prob.
LNDST	−2.968899	0.217799	−13.63135	0.0000
ER	0.080807	0.745257	0.108429	0.9140
LNFDI	0.092462	0.036359	2.543046	0.0131
LNGDP	1.125126	0.038716	29.06134	0.0000
BORDER	1.435678	0.026332	0.036359	0.0000
C	15.54534	1.609693	9.657330	0.0000

R^2	0.944905 Mean dependent var	4.941502
Adjusted R^2	0.941886 S.D. dependent var	2.713719
S.E. of regression	0.654193 Akaike info criterion	2.051127
Sum squared resid	31.24171 Schwarz criterion	2.202198
Log-likelihood	−74.99397 Hannan–Quinn criteria	2.111604
F statistic	312.9943 Durbin–Watson stat	1.283016
Prob (F statistic)	0.000000	

The empirical results obtained from panel OLS regression regarding import from Pakistan shows that regression model explains 94% variation in the model. This result indicates that the explanatory variables included in the equation explain 94% of the variation in the dependent variable. The *F* statistics is 312.99, and the probability of *F* statistics is 0.0000, which shows that the results are statistically significant and the null hypothesis of the independent variables having no effect on export is rejected. The results explain that distance, GDP and border is not statistically significant and have the expected sign except for the exchange rate. Distance is negatively related to import from Pakistan, which means greater distance reduces import from Pakistan. The assumption of the gravity model holds true in this case. GDP is positively related to import, which means higher production of goods and services increases imports from Pakistan. Closer border increases import to Pakistan. Exchange rate is positively related to import, which means a higher exchange rate increases import from Pakistan. Like exports, importing goods of Pakistan are also not sensitive to fluctuation in the exchange rate. The import items are crude oil, machinery and chemicals. The relationship between import and FDI are found complementary in this case.

Sri Lanka's Exports

Dependent Variable: LNEX

Method: Panel Least Squares

Sample: 2000–2016

Periods included: 17

Cross-sections included: 5

Total panel (balanced) observations: 85

Variable	Coefficient	Std. Error	*t*-Statistic	Prob.
LNDST	−3.235871	0.197091	−16.41819	0.0000
ER	−6.310296	1.906166	−3.310466	0.0016
BORDER	−1.905221	0.534270	−3.566024	0.0007
LNFDI	−0.350272	0.128734	−2.720892	0.0085
LNGDP	2.035353	0.120973	16.82486	0.0000
C	12.74477	2.032321	6.271041	0.0000

(Continued)

(*Continued*)

R^2	0.902024 Mean dependent var	3.313846
Adjusted R^2	0.893721 S.D. dependent var	3.474738
S.E. of regression	1.132779 Akaike info criterion	3.174990
Sum squared resid	75.70810 Schwarz criterion	3.375703
Log-likelihood	−97.18719 Hannan–Quinn criteria	3.254184
F statistic	108.6381 Durbin–Watson stat	0.864427
Prob(F statistic)	0.000000	

The result of the estimation for export of Sri Lanka shows a 90% variation in the model. This means that the independent variables included in the model explain 90% of the variation in the dependent variable. Here, the F statistics is found to be 108.63, and the probability of F statistics is 0.0000, which shows that the results are statistically significant and the null hypothesis of the independent variables having no effect on export is rejected. The results explain that distance, GDP and border are statistically significant and have the expected sign except for border and FDI. Distance is negatively related to export from Sri Lanka, which means greater distance reduces export from Sri Lanka. The result has confirmed the assumption of the gravity model. The major exporting items of Sri Lanka, e.g., tea and garments, are mainly sold in Russia, the European Union and UAE. In 2010 these three destinations accounted for about 62% of the total exports of Sri Lanka. GDP is positively related to export, which means higher production of goods and services increases export from Sri Lanka. Exchange rate is negatively related to export, which means higher exchange rate decreases import from Sri Lanka.

Sri Lanka was one of the early liberalized countries in terms of FDI and trade policy. The results of the model also suggest the verification of the gravity model. With the developed infrastructure and moderately cheaper labor force, the island country has been able to attract a huge amount of horizontal FDI, which in turn supplemented its export.

Sri Lanka's Imports

Dependent Variable: LNIM

Method: Panel Least Squares

Sample: 2000–2016

Periods included: 17

Cross-sections included: 5

Total panel (balanced) observations: 85

Variable	Coefficient	Std. Error	t-Statistic	Prob.
LNDST	−2.924462	0.253162	−11.55176	0.0000
ER	0.005625	2.448458	0.002297	0.9982
LNFDI	0.002490	0.165358	0.015060	0.9880
LNGDP	1.806651	0.155389	11.62664	0.0000
BORDER	−0.775891	0.686267	−1.130597	0.2628
C	6.088906	2.610504	2.332464	0.0231

R^2	0.827431 Mean dependent var	4.065226
Adjusted R^2	0.812806 S.D. dependent var	3.363036
S.E. of regression	1.455047 Akaike info criterion	3.675720
Sum squared resid	124.9126 Schwarz criterion	3.876432
Log-likelihood	−113.4609 Hannan–Quinn criteria	3.754914
F statistic	56.57836 Durbin–Watson stat	1.141898
Prob(F statistic)	0.000000	

The empirical results obtained from panel OLS regression pertaining to import from Sri Lanka shows that regression explains 82% variation in the model. Thus, the explanatory variables included in the equation explain 82% of the variation in the dependent variable. The F statistics is 56.56, and the probability of F statistics is 0.0000, which shows that the results are statistically significant and the null hypothesis of the independent variables having no effect on import is rejected. The results explain that distance and GDP are statistically significant and have the expected sign except for border and exchange rate. Distance is negatively related to import from Sri Lanka, which means greater distance reduces import to Sri Lanka. The assumption of gravity model is applicable here. Sri Lanka imported mostly from distant countries like the United States, Germany and UAE. Exchange rate is positively related to import, which means a higher exchange rate increases import from Sri Lanka. The import items are insensitive to the changes in the exchange rate. GDP is positively related to import, which means higher production of goods and services increases import from Sri Lanka. In the case of FDI, the relationship was found to be positive, which reflects its complementary relationship with import. Closer border decreases import from Sri Lanka.

5.5. Conclusion

The current chapter addressed the relationship between trade and FDI in the SAARC region. The gravity model was used to test the complementary or substitution relationship between trade and FDI in SAARC. The analysis was carried out for the top five investing countries in the SAARC nations excluding Afghanistan, Maldives and Bhutan. The lack of relevant data pertaining to these three countries barred us from considering them from the analysis.

The estimation results of the OLS panel regression found both complementary and supplementary relationship between trade and FDI in all the SAARC group of countries. The result shows a complementary relationship for all the selected countries with exception of Sri Lanka. The result finds that during 2000–2016, an inflow of FDI in the region through various multinational companies (MNCs) have helped to increase the trade, i.e., both exports and imports from the region. For all the selected countries, both the trade values and FDI inflows have increased substantially. India is a bigger market in size, and with a developed infrastructure and low wage rate, it has been able to attract the highest amount of FDI in the region. Other economies in the region are comparatively smaller in size and due to poor infrastructure, they could attract only a lower amount of FDI. Following the theory, it can be assumed that most of the FDI flow in these smaller economies were vertical in nature, which has positively impacted their trade. The implications of the distance and existence of a border between two trading nations were found to be different. The exchange rate impacting trade and FDI between the two countries was also found to be different for different countries.

For exports of Bangladesh, the proposition of gravity model was not found to be applicable while it was true in case of imports. Similarly, Indian imports rejected the gravity model while it is accepted in the case of export. The same result was also found in the case of Pakistan where exports rejected the gravity model, but it was found to be applicable for imports. Both exports and imports of Nepal and Sri Lanka confirmed the assumption that longer distance reduces trade.

Thus, it can be concluded from the results that for SAARC group of countries both complementary and supplementary relationship exists between trade and FDI. In the case of some countries, the relationship was found to be complimentary while for some others the relationship was supplementary.

After having analyzed the complementary or substitution relationship between trade and FDI in SAARC region, a major question still remains regarding the causality between them, i.e., whether trade follows the FDI or it is FDI which is following trade in this region. This issue is taken up in our next chapter.

References

Amiti, M., David, G., & Katharine, W. (2000). Foreign Direct Investment and Trade: Substitutes or Complements, Unpublished paper of the University of Melbourne.

Anderson, J. E. (1979). A Theoretical Foundation for the Gravity Equation. *The American Economic Review*, 63, 106–116.

Belderbos, R., & Sleuwaegen, L. (1998). Tariff Jumping DFI and Export Substitution: Japanese electronics firms in Europe. *International Journal of Industrial Organization*, 16(5), 601–638.

Bergstrand, J. H. (1985). The Gravity Equation in International Trade: Some Microeconomic Foundations and Empirical Evidence. *The Review of Economics and Statistics*, 67(3), 474–481.

Bergstrand, J. H., Egger, P., & Larch, M. (2008). The New Expats: Economic Determinants of Bilateral Expatriate, FDI, and International Trade Flows, Working Paper, University of Notre Dame.

Bhagwati, J., & Panagariya, A. (2004). The Muddles over Outsourcing. *Journal of Economic Perspectives*, 18(4), 93–114.

Board of Investment (2010), Foreign Direct Investment in Bangladesh (1971–2010), Prime Minister's office, Government of Bangladesh.

Braconier, H., Norbäck, P. J., & Urban, D. (2005). Reconciling the Evidence on the Knowledge-capital Model. *Review of International Economics*, 13(4), 770–786.

Brainard S.L. (1997). An Empirical Assessment of the Proximity-Concentration Trade-off between Multinationals Sales and Trade. *American Economic Review*, 8, 520–544.

Brainard, S. L. (1993). A Simple Theory of Multinational Corporations and Trade with a Tradeoff between Proximity and Concentration, Working Paper No 4269, NBER.

Chaisrisawatsuk, S., & Chaisrisawatsuk, W. (2007). Imports, Exports, and Foreign Direct Investment Interactions and Their Effects. In *ESCAP, Towards Coherent Policy Frameworks: Understanding Trade and Investment Linkages–A Study by the Asia-Pacific Research and Training Network on Trade*, Chapter IV. United Nations.

Clausing, K. A. (2000). Does Multinational Activity Displace Trade? *Economic Inquiry*, 38(2), 190–205.

Deardorff, A. (1997) Determinants of Bilateral Trade: Does Gravity Work in a Classical World? In *The Regionalization of the World Economy*, ed., Jeffrey Frankel, Chicago, IL: University of Chicago Press.

DIPP (2013). *SIA New Letters*, Various Issues, DIPP New Delhi.

Fontagné, L. (1999). *Foreign Direct Investment and International Trade: Complements or Substitutes?* OECD Publishing.

Gopinath, M., Pick, D., & Vasavada, U. (1999). The Economics of Foreign Direct Investment and Trade with an Application to the Us Food Processing Industry. *American Journal of Agricultural Economics*, 81(2), 442–452.

Graham, E. (1999). On the Relationship among Direct Investment and International Trade in the Manufacturing Sector: Empirical Results from the U.S. and Japan, Working Paper, Institute of International Economics, Washington DC.

Hailu, Z. A. (2010). Impact of Foreign Direct Investment on Trade of African Countries. *International Journal of Economics and Finance*, 2(3), 122.

Helpman E., Melitz M., & Yeaple S. (2003). Export versus FDI, NBER Working Paper No. 9439.

IIFT (2009). Measures to Boost Indian Tea Exports — An Analysis of Competitiveness Issues, Unpublished report Submitted to Tea Board of India.

Jain, R., & Singh, J. (2009). Trade Pattern in SAARC Countries: Emerging Trends and Issues, Reserve Bank of India. *Occasional Papers*, 30(3), 73–117.

Khan, S. R., Yusuf, M., Bohkari, S., & Aziz, S. (2007). Quantifying Informal Trade between Pakistan and India. *The Challenges and Potential of Pakistan India Trade*. World Bank.

Krugman, P. (1983). "The New Theories of International Trade and the Multinational Enterprise", in Charles P. Kindleberger and David Audretch (eds.), *The Multinational Corporation in the 1980s*. Cambridge, Mass: MIT Press, pp. 57–73.

Lin, A-l. (1995). Trade Effects of Foreign Direct Investment: Evidence for Taiwan with Four ASEAN Countries, *Weltwirtschaftliches Archive*, 4, 737–747.

Marchant, M. A., Cornell, D. N., & Koo, W. (2002). International Trade and Foreign Direct Investment: Substitutes or Complements?, *Journal of Agricultural and Applied Economics*, 34(2), 289–302.

Moazzem, K. G. (2013, March). Regional Investment Cooperation in South Asia: Policy Issues. In *Presentation at the conference organized by Research and Information Systems and Commonwealth Secretariat in New Delhi, March*.

Muni, S. D. (1992). *India and Nepal: A changing relationship* (p. 49). New Delhi: Konark Publishers.

National Board of Trade (2008). The Relationship between International Trade and Foreign Direct Investments for Swedish Multinational Enterprises, National Board of Trade, Sweden.

Norbäck, P.-J., Urban, D., & Westerberg, S. (2007). Gravity Estimation for Multinational Enterprises: An application to the GATT/WTO Puzzle, RIIE Working Paper.

Overend, C., Connor, J. M., & Salin, V. (1997). Foreign Direct Investment and US Exports of Processed Foods: Complements or Substitutes?, Paper presented at the Foreign Direct Investment and Processed Food Trade. Conference Proceedings of the NCR-182, Organization, and Performance of World Food Systems, Oklahoma State University, Stillwater, OK, 31–56.

Pfaffermayr, M. (1996). Foreign Outward Direct Investment and Exports in Austrian Manufacturing: Substitutes or Complements?, *Weltwirtschaftliches Archiv, 132*(3), 501–522.

Rajeev Jain, & J. B. Singh (2009) "Trade Pattern in SAARC Countries: Emerging Trends and Issues," Reserve Bank of India, Occasional Papers, Vol. 30, No. 3.

Stone, S. F., & Jeon, B. N. (2000). Foreign Direct Investment and Trade in the Asia-Pacific Region: Complementarity, Distance and Regional Economic Integration. *Journal of Economic Integration, 15*(3), 460–484.

Tinbergen, J. (1962). Shaping the World Economy; Suggestions for an International Economic Policy. The Twentieth Century Fundd, New York.

UNCTAD (1996). World Investment Report, UNCTAD, Geneva.

Vernon, R. (1966). International Investment and International Trade in The Product Cycle. *The Quarterly Journal of Economics*, 190–207.

World Bank (2006). India-Bangladesh Bilateral Trade and Potential Free Trade Agreement, Bangladesh Development Series, Paper No-13. World Bank, Dhaka, Bangladesh.

Chapter 6

Causal Relation between Trade and Investment in the SAARC Region

This chapter analyzes the relationship between FDI and trade in the SAARC countries using co-integration and Granger causality tests applied to panel data to understand whether trade and FDI are complementary or substitute each other, i.e., whether a greater FDI inflow held by a nation is associated with decreases or increases in its exports and imports. The results reveal that in the case of SAARC region, higher FDI inflows leads to a higher trade volume. The results also indicate a unidirectional causality from FDI to trade, which could be a good tool to prioritize the allocation of resources across sectors to promote FDI to increase international trade.

6.1. Introduction

As the continuously growing trend in businesses worldwide is to globalize, firms would benefit from exploring new markets to expand their operations in order to maintain global competitiveness through FDI and trade (Merchant, 2016). In this era of globalization, emerging markets are often the main target for investment and trade (Welsh *et al.*, 2006; Fornes & Butt-Philipp, 2011; Paul, 2016; Jadhav *et al.*, 2016).

The traditional theories of FDI maintain that there can be two-way relationships between trade and FDI (see for instance Brainard, 1997; Fontagne, 1999; Helpman *et al.*, 2003). In the initial stage, foreign markets are generally catered through exports. Once the foreign firms gain knowledge about the economic and political behavior of the domestic market, they establish production subsidiaries in the domestic market. The subsidiary of the foreign firm may export to other countries. Thus, it has been asserted that there can be a two-way causal linkage between trade and FDI, i.e., trade will first cause FDI and later FDI may eventually lead to trade. The causality relationship between FDI and trade definitively impacts the decision-making process. The literature on FDI and trade identify two major directions: one is whether FDI determines the international trade or whether FDI substitutes or a complements trade.

Though SAARC countries are not a homogeneous group of countries, there appear to be some common dimensions in the recent upsurge of foreign direct investment (FDI) and trade from multinational enterprises (MNEs) from developed countries and from other emerging economies. MNEs are increasingly looking for expanding their businesses internationally to achieve global competitive advantage (Mudambi & Mudambi, 2002; Bhasin & Paul, 2016). As the seminal theoretical work OLI (ownership, location and internalization) paradigm explains, MNEs carry out FDI to take advantage of their ownership (O) specific advantages in foreign markets characterized by specific features also known as location (L) specific, recognizing and executing the most suitable mode of entry relating these two sets of advantages via internalization (I) (Dunning, 2009).

FDI and trade play an important role in the improvement of an economy as it bridges the gap between the desired and the actual level of investment and offers a variety of goods and services at competitive prices to the host nation (Noorbakhsh *et al.*, 2001; Hayami, 2001). FDI plays an important role in the economic development of a country by bringing non-debt-creating capital flows, transferring new technology into the host country, and generating more employment opportunities in the host economy. FDI also helps related industries by creating backward and forward linkages within the host economy (Alfaro & Rodriguez-Clare, 2004; Ho & Rashid, 2011; Javorcik, 2004). Besides, FDI and trade boost the productivity of host countries by promoting competition in the domestic market (Caves, 1974). FDI also enhances tax revenues, which are used by the government on different development activities like building basic infrastructure and human capital for the growth of industries (Adhikary, 2011; Bhavan *et al.*, 2011; Azam, 2010).

It is in this context that the main objective of this chapter is to investigate whether any causal relationship exists between international trade and FDI in the SAARC countries. The remainder of the chapter is organized as follows. The next section reviews the theoretical and empirical literature related to FDI and trade linkages. The subsequent session is designed for a discussion on the data and methodology applied in the empirical part of the chapter. Next, the results are presented and, finally, the conclusion and policy implication is discussed.

6.2. Research Insights

As per factor proportion theory propounded by Heckscher (1919) and Ohlin (1933), it is the differences in endowments of factors of production that explain trade. They stated that countries would export goods and services that utilized greater quantities of their relatively abundant factors, and import other goods and services (that is, those that were relatively scarce factors). This model suggests that international trade of goods involves an indirect exchange of factors between the trading countries. The theory also suggests that, even under the assumption that factors of production are perfectly immobile between countries, factors do move between countries in the form of exports and imports of commodities.

Further, Mundell (1957) maintained that tariff protection would lead to perfect substitution between FDI and international trade. He argued that international trade and the international mobility of factors of production, which includes FDI, are substitutes rather than compliments for each other where there are barriers to trade.

Trade impediments stimulate factor movements and that increased impediments to factor movements stimulate trade.

Helpman (1984) and Helpman and Krugman (1985) argued that the degree of specialization is a positive function of relative factor endowments. If there are significant differences in factor endowments, the capital-abundant country tends to export services into the labor-abundant country in exchange for finished varieties of a differentiated good or a homogeneous good. Thus, FDI generates complementary trade flows from the labor-rich country.

Ethier (1986) asserted that both a greater uncertainty faced by the firm and a greater similarity in factor endowments between countries make FDI more likely, leading to two-way FDI and a relatively higher intra-industry and intra-firm trade. Similarly, Barrios (1997) found that, for countries having common border engaged in a process of economic integration, both intermediate imports and exports of the final good would lead to higher integration.

Some of the recent theories have divided the motives for undertaking FDI into three major categories; first, the horizontal motives, second, the vertical motivations (see Markusen, 1984 and Markusen and Venables, 1998 for horizontal motives and see Helpman, 1984; Helpman and Krugman, 1985 for vertical motives). And finally, the knowledge-capital model as proposed by Markusen and Maskus (2001), which combines both the horizontal and vertical models into a single model. Theoretically, horizontal FDI replicates the whole production process in the foreign country and thereby avoids trade costs and leads to a supplementary relationship with trade. On the other hand, vertical FDI and trade are complementary because vertical FDI is driven by the distance of production costs rather than trade costs. In the case of vertical FDI, the same product is produced in different countries.

Based on the above theoretical foundation, several researchers have empirically tested the casual linkages between trade and investment. Rubio and Munoz (1999) analyzes the causal relationship between outward FDI and exports in an empirical analysis. The results found the existence of a long-run Granger causality from outward FDI to exports during the reference period. However, no short-run Granger causality was found between these two variables. The authors argued that with the increase in the capital outflow in the liberalization process might lead to higher export.

Pacheco-Lopez (2005) analyzed the liberalization of FDI in Mexico since the late 1980s and its relationships with exports and imports using the Granger causality method. The results found bidirectional Granger causality between exports and FDI. The paper also explored that FDI has a close relationship with imports in the case of Mexico. With the increase in FDI, the import content has been intensified.

Lee and Song (2008) used Granger causality method to analyze trade and FDI relationship in Korea. The analysis used annual data for the period 1970–2004. The research found two-way linkages between trade and FDI. The results showed that trade led to higher FDI between Korea and the United States and China while FDI caused trade between Korea and Japan.

Kiran (2010) investigated the relationship between trade and FDI in the case of Turkey by using Granger causality methodology. The paper considered a time period from 1998 to 2004. The author found no causal relationship exists between FDI and trade in Turkey. The results suggested improvement of the educated labor force and developing a financial system and political instability, before allowing foreign investment.

Shaikh (2010) used quarterly time series data from 1998 to 2009 to examine the causal relationship between FDI, international trade and economic growth in Pakistan. The results found a positive impact of FDI on the trade growth of Pakistan. The results also found the existence of two-way causal connections between economic growth, export and FDI, with unidirectional of import to export and FDI.

Rahman (2011) analyzed the relationship between foreign investment and international trade in Bangladesh covering the time period between 1972 and 2007. The analysis also used Granger causality model for the analysis. The results showed no causality between trade and FDI in Bangladesh.

Cho (2013) examined the relationship between FDI and international trade for India with four East Asian countries, namely China,

Japan, Korea and Singapore. The research also covered four more countries for the analysis, which are also major trading partners with India. These countries are the United States, UK, Germany and the Netherlands. The analysis used quarterly data for the time period from 2004 to 2012. In Korea–India, Japan–India and Singapore–India bilateral relationships, the causality between trade and FDI could not be found. As against in the cases of United States–India, UK–India and Germany–India, the relationship was found to be two-way and one-way causality, respectively.

Sharma and Kaur (2013) conducted a comparative study between India and China for the causal relationship between trade and FDI. The study employed Granger causality method using annual data for the time period between 1976 and 2011. The results found unidirectional causality running from FDI to imports and FDI to exports in the case of China. The paper also established the existence of bidirectional causality between imports and exports in the case of China. But for India, the authors found bidirectional causality between FDI and imports, FDI and exports, and exports and imports.

From the above, it is clear that the available literature is unambiguous in explaining the casual relationship. Some studies have reported that trade is influencing higher FDI inflows while some have advocated about the converse, i.e., high inflow of FDI is leading to a higher volume of trade. Further, an interaction between FDI and trade has become more complicated with the trend of economic integration (see Cho, 2013 for more details). Both the existence and non-existence of causal relationships were reported by different studies. Further, only a few studies were conducted for SAARC member countries. Moreover, no research has studied the causal relationship between trade and FDI for the SAARC region as a whole. It is this lacuna the current chapter is going to bridge.

6.3. Econometric Methodology

6.3.1. *Data sources*

The dataset consists of panel observations for eight SAARC countries over the 1991–2016 period. We have used UN COMTRADE for collecting export and import data for all the selected countries. UN COMTRADE was accessed from the World Integrated Trade Solution (WITS) online database. Data for FDI inflows in the selected countries were extracted from UN statistics. Data on FDI and trade are in US dollars at current prices and current exchange rates in millions. Econometric software E-views 9.5 is used to analyze the econometric model.

6.3.2. The model[1]

In order to analyze the long-term relationship between trade and FDI in the SAARC region the choice of the appropriate technique is an important factor. Co-integration is the most appropriate technique to identify the long-term relationship between FDI and trade. This paper used three main econometric methodologies to identify the long-term relationship between FDI and trade. First, panel unit-root tests are undertaken to identify whether data is stationary, non-stationary or integrated at the same order. Second, if the data is integrated as the same order the co-integration test is used with the methods FMOLS and DOLS. Finally, panel Granger causality test is performed.

The concept of co-integration is described as a systematic co-movement among two or more variables in the long term. According to Engle and Granger (1987), if X and Y are both non-stationary, it was expected that a linear combination of X and Y is a random step. However, the two variables can have the propriety that a particular combination of them $Z = X — By$ is stationary. If this propriety is true, we say that X and Y are co-integrated.

6.3.3. Panel co-integration

According to recent literature in econometrics, it is believed that the panel dataset possesses several other advantages over cross-sectional or time-series dataset to test unit roots and co-integration. Panel data model usually gives a larger number of data points, increasing the

---

[1] This section is largely drawn from *Abbes et al.* (2014).

degrees of freedom and reducing the collinearity among the explanatory variables, and hence improving the efficiency of econometric estimates. It allows analysis of a number of important economic questions that cannot be tackled by cross-section or time-series data while becoming more informative (Jadhav, 2012, 2016).

The first step is to test the unit roots panel and the second is the co-integration tests in the panel. For the countries in our empirical study, heterogeneity may arise due to differences in the degree of economic and development conditions of each country. To ensure wide applicability of any co-integration panel test, it is important to take into account as much as possible heterogeneity between group members. Pedroni (1999, 2004) has developed a method of the co-integration panel based on residues that can take into account the heterogeneity in individual effects, the slope coefficients and individual linear trends between countries. Pedroni (2004) considers the following type of regression:

$$y_{it} = \alpha_i + \delta_{it} + \beta_i X_{it} + e_{it}. \tag{6.1}$$

We consider for each panel, time series y_{it} and X_{it} for the members $I = 1,..., N$ and for periods of time $t = 1,..., T$. The variables y_{it} and X_{it} are supposed to be integrated of order 1, denoted by $I(I)$ the parameters α_i and δ_{it}. They allow the opportunity to observe the individual effects and individual linear trends, respectively.

The β_i slope coefficients are allowed to vary from one member to another, so in general, the co-integration vectors may be heterogeneous among the panel members. Pedroni (1997) proposes seven statistics to test the null hypothesis of no co-integration in heterogeneous panels. These tests include two types of tests. The first is the co-integration tests panel (within-dimension). Within test dimensions consist using four statistics, namely panel v-statistic, panel ρ-statistic, panel PP-statistic, and panel ADF-statistic. These statistics pool the autoregressive coefficients across different members for the unit root tests on the estimated residues, and the last three test statistics are based on the "between" dimension (the "group"). These tests are group ρ, group PP and group ADF statistics.

6.3.4. *Estimating the long-run co-integration relationship in a panel context*

After confirmation of the existence of a co-integration relationship between the series, it must be followed by the estimation of the long-term relationship. There are different estimators available to estimate a vector co-integration panel data, including with and between groups such as OLS estimates, fully modified OLS (FMOLS) estimators and estimators dynamic OLS (DOLS).

6.3.5. *Panel Granger causality*

Panel co-integration method tests whether the existence or absence of a long-run relationship between FDI and trade for the seven panels. It doesn't indicate the direction of causality. When co-integration exists among the variables, the causal relationship should be modeled within a dynamic error correction model (Engle and Granger 1987).

The main purpose of our chapter is to establish the causal linkages between FDI and trade. The Granger causality tests will be based on the following regressions:

$$(1-L)\begin{bmatrix} \text{FDI}_{it} \\ \text{Trade}_{it} \end{bmatrix} = \begin{bmatrix} a_{i\,\text{FDI}} \\ a_{i\,\text{Trade}} \end{bmatrix} + \sum_{i=1}^{P}(1-L)\begin{bmatrix} \vartheta_{11ip} & \vartheta_{12ip} \\ \vartheta_{21ip} & \vartheta_{22ip} \end{bmatrix}\begin{bmatrix} \text{FDI}_{it-p} \\ \text{Trade}_{it-p} \end{bmatrix}$$

$$+ \begin{bmatrix} \beta_{\text{FDI}i} \\ \beta_{\text{Trade}i} \end{bmatrix}\text{ECT}_{t-1} + \begin{bmatrix} \varepsilon_{1t} \\ \varepsilon_{2t} \end{bmatrix},$$

Where ECT_{t-1} is the error-correction term, p denotes the lag length and $(1-L)$ is the first difference operator and ECT_{t-1} stands for the lagged error-correction term derived from the long-run co-integration relationship. An error correction model enables one to distinguish between the long-run and short-run Granger causality. The short-term dynamics are captured by the individual coefficients of the lagged terms. Statistical significance of the coefficients of each explanatory variable is used to test for the short-run Granger causality while the significance of the coefficients of ECT_{t-1} gives information about long-run causality. It is also desirable to test whether the two sources of causation are jointly significant.

6.4. Estimation Results

The general specification of the model which we estimate can be written as follows:

$$y_{it} = \alpha_i + \beta_i X_{it} + e_{it},$$

where y is the FDI of country i, for the period t, X is also the trade of country i, given at the period t and e_{it} is an error term. This equation is considered as a balanced long-term relationship if it has co-integration relations. The data must then be integrated in the same order. We will test the stationarity and the relationship of long-term series of FDI and trade. The technical unit root and cointegration panel data require a minimum of homogeneity in order to draw more general conclusions.

The empirical results (Table 6.1) obtained from the unit root test indicates that all statistics are not significant at the 1% level for both variables Trade and FDI. After differentiation into first-degree data,

Table 6.1:   Unit Root Test for the Variables

Variable		LLC	IPS	MW-ADF Fisher Chi-square	MW-PP Fisher Chi-square
FDI	Level	2.19(0.98)	2.22(0.98)	10.24(0.85)	12.38(0.71)
Trade		3.84(0.99)	6.18(1.00)	1.01(1.00)	0.65(1.00)
FDI	Frist Difference	−4.41(0.00)***	−7.91(0.00)***	88.90(0.00)***	164.727(0.00)***
Trade		−5.82(0.00)***	−7.04(0.00)***	79.23(0.00)***	142.80 (0.00)***

Note: Against each variable, the first row represents the coefficient followed by *p* value in the parenthesis.
*Significant at 10%; **Significant at 5%; ***Significant at 1%.

we notice a significant way that all data are stationary for both variables. These results led us to a logical way to test for the presence or absence of a long-term relationship between GDP and FDI by applying co-integration.

6.5. Co-integration

Co-integration requires that all the variables are integrated of the same order. The results of the panel unit root test indicate that GDP and FDI are first-order integrated. We proceed to test co-integration panel by relying on tests. The results are as follows:

The empirical results in Table 6.2 show that both the within and between dimension panel co-integration test statistics. These statistics are based on averages of the individual autoregressive coefficients associated with the unit root tests of the residuals for each country in the panel. These results suggest that in all panel datasets there is a co-integration long-run relationship between FDI and trade for our panel of continents. In this step, we estimate the long-term relationships using FMOLS methods and DOLS estimators proposed by Pedroni, Kao and Chiang and Mark and Sul.

Table 6.2: Co-Integration Test

Methods	Within Dimension (Panel Statistics)			Between Dimension (Individuals Statistics)		
	Test	Statistics	Prob.	Test	Statistics	Prob.
Pedroni (1999)	Panel v-statistic	5.47	0.00	Group rho-statistic	−2.64	0.00
	Panel rho-statistic	−3.08	0.00	Group PP-statistic	−3.56	0.00
	Panel PP-statistic	−2.14	0.01	Group ADF statistic	−3.46	0.00
	Panel ADF-Statistic	−4.47	0.00			
Pedroni (2004)	Panel v-statistic	3.57	0.00			
Weighted Statistics	Panel rho-statistic	−4.07	0.00			
	Panel PP-statistic	−3.79	0.00			
	Panel ADF-Statistic	3.72	0.00			

Table 6.3:   FMOLS and DOLS Estimation

Dependent Variable	Independent Variables	
Trade	FDI	FDI
	FMOLS	DOLS
	17.27 (0.00)***	18.74 (0.00)***
	R^2 0.87	R^2 0.94

Note: Against each variable, the first row represents the coefficient followed by p value in the parenthesis.
*Significant at 10%; **Significant at 5%; ***Significant at 1%.

6.6. The FMOLS and DOLS Estimations

Having established that the variables are stationary and exhibit long-run co-integration panel in the previous subsections, we now estimate the long-run impact of FDI on trade of SAARC countries. The results of panel method FMOLS are similar to DOLS estimators; all results are presented in Table 6.3.

The tables report the long-run elasticity estimates from FMOLS and DOLS (coefficients can be interpreted as elasticity because the variables are expressed in natural logarithms). All of the estimated coefficients indicate that trade is correlated positively and significantly with FDI at the 1% level. Overall, the results of FDI and trade regression panel demonstrate a strong long-term relationship between both and show the importance of FDI for increasing trade in the analysis of SAARC regions.

The results obtained for all panel of SAARC countries indicate that a 1% increase in foreign investment increases the trade by 17.27 and 18.74, respectively, for FMOLS and DOLS model. These results indicate that the flow of FDI has a positive and significant long-run effect on trade in our overall.

6.7. Granger Causality Test

The existence of co-integration implies the existence of causality at least in one direction. Having found that there is a long-run relationship between FDI and trade, the next step is done to objectively test the causality between these variables by using the panel Granger causality test.

This chapter focuses on the relationship between FDI and trade. A Granger causality analysis is carried out in order to assess whether there is any potential predictability power of one indicator for the other.

The results of the Granger causality test for all panels are summarized in the following table. It should be noted that optimal lag was established using the Akaike and Schwarz information criteria.

Null Hypothesis	F-Statistic	Prob
Trade does not Granger cause FDI	14.51	0.00
FDI does not Granger cause trade	74	0.00

From the Granger causality test results in the table, null hypothesis is shown. Trade does not cause FDI is rejected for all panels at 10% level. This suggests that trade and FDI depend upon each other in the long run following Granger causality. The results indicate that unidirectional causality exists between FDI and trade for the SAARC region.

6.8. Conclusion

In order to capture whether the trade is leading a higher volume of FDI inflows or FDI is enhancing the trade volume, the current chapter investigated if any causal relationship exists between trade and FDI for SAARC countries. The panel Granger causality method was employed to analyze the relationship for the time period from 1991 to 2016.

First, panel unit root tests are performed to determine whether the data series are stationary in levels or require first differentiation. The findings show that all statistics are not significant at the level for both variables trade and FDI. After differentiation into first-degree data, we notice a significant way that all data are stationary for both variables. These results led us to a logical way to test for the presence or absence of a long-term relationship between GDP and FDI by applying cointegration. The FMOLS and DOLS tests confirm the long-term equilibrium relationship between FDI and trade.

The result reveals that in the case of SAARC region higher FDI inflows are leading to higher trade volume. Thus the relationship between FDI and trade are complementary, which give an indication that the SAARC region has intra-industry trade. This result also rejects tariff-jumping hypothesis, which indicates that FDI in SAARAC countries is not coming in because of high tariff and non-tariff barriers. It is motivated by a low level of production cost and again re-exported to another country. The results also indicate a unidirectional causality from FDI to trade, which could be a good tool to prioritize the allocation of resources across sectors to promote FDI to increase international trade. These results may help a government to establish priorities regarding the assignment of the resources for national strategies to increase trade by increasing FDI into their respective countries.

References

Adhikary, B. K. (2011). FDI, Trade Openness, Capital Formation, and Economic Growth in Bangladesh: A Linkage Analysis. *International Journal of Business and Management*, 6(1), 10–21.

Alfaro, L., & Rodriguez-Clare, A. (2004). Multinationals and Linkages: Evidence from Latin America. *Economia*, 4(2), 113–170.

Azam, M. (2010). An Empirical Analysis of the Impacts of Exports and Foreign Direct Investment on Economic Growth in South Asia. *Interdisciplinary Journal of Contemporary Research in Business*, 2(7), 249.

Barrios, S. (1997). *Inversióndirectaextranjer y especializacióncomercial en los paísesperiféricos.* Documento de Trabajo 97-16, FEDEA, Madrid.

Bhavan, T., Xu, C., & Zhong, C. (2011). Determinants and Growth Effect of FDI in South Asian Economies: Evidence from a Panel Data Analysis. *International Business Research*, 4(1).

Brainard S. L. (1997). An Empirical Assessment of the Proximity-Concentration Trade-off between Multinationals Sales and Trade. *American Economic Review*, 8, 520–544.

Cho, C. (2013). The Causal Relationship between Trade and FDI: Implication for India and East Asian Countries, KIEP Working Paper, 13-06, Korea.

Engle, R. F. & Granger, C. (1987). Co-integration and Error-correction: Representation, Estimation and Testing. *Econometrica*, 49(4), 1057–1072.

Ethier, W. J. (1986). The Multinational Firm. *Quarterly Journal of Economics*, 101, 805–833.

Fontagné L. (1999). Foreign Direct Investment and International Trade: Complements Substitutes? OECD Science, Technology and Industry Working Papers, 1999/03, OECD Publishing.

Fornes, G., & Butt-Philipp, A. (2011). ChineseMNEs and Latin America: A Review. *International Journal of Emerging Markets*, 6(2), 98–117.

Granger, C. (1969). Investigating Causal Relations by Econometric Models and Cross-Spectral Methods. *Econometrica,* 37, 24–36.

Hayami, Y. (2001). *Development Economics: From the Poverty to the Wealth of Nations*, Oxford: University Press.

Hecksher, E. F. (1919). The Effects of Foreign Trade on the Distribution of Income. *EkonomicTidskrift,* XXI (in Swedish). [Reprinted in translation by Svend and Nita Laursen (1949) in *Readings in the Theory of International Trade*, Howard S. Ellish & Lloyd A. Metzler, eds., Philadelphia: The Blakiston Company.]

Helpman, E., (1984). A Simple Theory of International Trade with Multinational Corporations. *Journal of Political Economy*, 92, 451–471.

Helpman, E. & Krugman, P. R. (1985). *Market Structure and Foreign Trade: Increasing Returns, Imperfect Competition, and the International Economy*, Cambridge: The MIT Press.

Helpman, E., Melitz M., & Yeaple S. (2003). Export versus FDI, NBER Working Paper, No. 9439.

Ho, C.S., & Rashid H.A (2011). Macroeconomic and Country Specific Determinants of FDI. *The Business Review*, 18(1), 219–226.

Jadhav, P., (2012). Determinants of Foreign Direct Investment in BRICS Economies. Analysis of Economic, Institutional and Political Factors. *Procedia Social and Behavioral Sciences*, 37, 5–14.

Jadhav, P., & Katti, V. (2012). Institutional and Political Determinants of Foreign Direct Investment. Evidence from BRICS Economies. *Poverty and Public Policy*, 4(3), 49–57.

Jadhav, P., Katti, V., & Choudhury, R. (2016). Trends, Determinants and Challenges of Foreign Direct Investment in Emerging Markets. *Trade,*

Investment, and Economic Development in Asia: Empirical and Policy Issues, New York: Routledge, pp. 235–246.

Javorcik, B. S. (2004). Does Foreign Direct Investment Increase the Productivity of Domestic Firms? In Search of Spillovers through Backward Linkages. *American Economic Review*, 94, 605–627.

Johansen, S. (1988). Statistical Analysis of Cointegration Vectors. *Journal of Economic Dynamic and Control*, 12, 231–254.

Johansen, S., (1991). Estimation and Hypothesis Testing of Co-integration Vectors in Gaussian Vector Autoregressive Models. *Econometrica*, 59(6), 1551–1580.

Johansen, S., & Juselius, K. (1990). Maximum Likelihood Estimation and Inference on Co-integration with Application to the Demand for Money. *Oxford Bulletin of Economics and Statistics*, 52, 169–210.

Kiran, B. (2011). Causal Links between Foreign Direct Investment and Trade in Turkey. *International Journal of Economics and Finance*, 3(2), 150–158.

Lee, J. H., & Song, J. S. (2008). Is There a Two-Way Linkage Between Trade and FDI? Evidence from Korea's Major Trading Partners. *International Area Studies*, 3, 25–41.

Markusen, J., (1984). Multinationals, Multi-Plant Economies, and the Gains from Trade. *Journal of International Economics*, 16(3–4), 205–226.

Markusen, J., & Maskus, K. (2001). General Equilibrium Approaches to the Multinational Firm: A Review of Theory and Evidence, NBER Working Paper No. 8334.

Markusen, J., & Venables, A. (1998). Multinational Firms and the New Trade Theory. *Journal of International Economics*, 46(2), 183–203.

Merchant, H. (2016). *Handbook of Research on Emerging Markets*, London, UK: Elgar Publishing.

Mudambi, R., & Mudambi, S. (2002). Diversification and Market Entry Choices in the Context of Foreign Direct Investment. *International Business Review*, 11(1), 35–55.

Mundell, R. A. (1957). International Trade and Factor Mobility. *American Economic Review*, 47, 321–335.

Noorbakhsh, F., Alberto, P., & Ali, Y. (2001). Human Capital and FDI inflows in Developing Countries: New Empirical Evidence. *World Development*, 29(9), 1593–1610.

Ohlin, B. (1933). *Interregional and International Trade*, Cambridge: Harvard University Press.

Pacheco-Lopez, P. (2005). Foreign Direct Investment, Exports, and Imports in Mexico. *The World Economy*, 28(8), 1157–1172.

Paul, J. (2016). "The Rise of China: What, When, Where and Why? *The International Trade Journal,* 30(3), 207–222.

Pearce, I., & Rowen, D. C. (1966). A Framework for Research into the Real Effects of International Capital Movements. In *Essays in Honour of Marco Fanno* (2 vols.), T. Bagiott ed., Italy: Cedam, Padova.

Pedroni, P. (2004). Panel cointegration: asymptotic and finite sample properties of pooled time series tests with an application to the PPP hypothesis. *Econometric Theory*, 20(3), 597–625.

Pedroni, P. (1999). Critical values for cointegration tests in heterogeneous panels with multiple regressors. *Oxford Bulletin of Economics and Statistics*, 61(S1), 653–670.

Perron, P. (1989). The Great Crush, the Oil Price Shock, and the Unit Root Hypothesis. *Econometrica*, 57, 1361–1401, available at http://www.jastor.org/stable/1913712.

Rahman, M. Z. (2011). An Empirical Study on the Relationship between Foreign Investment and International Trade in Bangladesh. *International Journal of Financial Research*, 2(2), 33–39.

Rubino, O. B. & Munoz, M. M. (1999). Foreign Direct Investment and Trade: A causality Analysis. *Open Economies Review*, 12(3), 305–323.

Shaikh, F. M. (2010). Causality relationship between foreign direct investment, trade and economic growth in Pakistan. In Paper presented at *International Conference on Applied Economic Canadian Center of Science and Education*, pp. 82–89.

Sharma, R., & Mandeep, K. (2013). Causal Links between Foreign Direct Investments and Trade: A Comparative Study of India and China. *Eurasian Journal of Business and Economics*, 6(11), 75–91.

Stock, H. J., & Watson, W. M. (1988). Variable Trends in Economic Time-Series. *Journal of Economic Perspectives*, 2(3), 147–174.

Strazicich, M. C., Lee, J., & Day, E. (2004). Are Income Converging among OECD Countries? Time Series Evidence with Two Structural Breaks. *Journal of Macroeconomics*, 26, 131–145.

Welsh, D. H., Alon, I., & Falbe, C. M. (2006). "An Examination of International Retail Franchising in Emerging Markets. *Journal of Small Business Management*, 44(1), 130.

Chapter 7

A SUR Analysis of Investment and Institutional Variables

Having tested the Granger causality between trade and FDI in the SAARC region in the last chapter, the current chapter makes an attempt to understand the relationship in a little deeper. The chapter tries to capture the role of various institutional variables proposed by Heritage Foundation in promoting FDI in the SAARC region. The chapter applies SUR model to investigate the relationship and role of these variables.

7.1. Introduction

In the preceding chapter, on the basis of the Granger causality test, it was found that there is no causal relationship between trade and FDI in the SAARC region. It was also found that except for India for the majority of SAARC countries, liberal FDI policy has not helped in attracting FDI. It is possible that apart from trade and policy variables, there may be other institutional factors that play an important role in attracting higher FDI inflows (Aleksynska & Havrylchyk, 2013). This is equally true for both developed and developing countries, even though the characteristics of the institutions differ among the regions and countries. The institutional factors like business freedom and investment freedom of the host country highly affect its FDI flows.

An institution is defined as "a system of rules, beliefs, norms, and organizations that together generate a regularity of (social) behaviour" (Greif, 2006). This definition of institution differs from that of North (1990) who considers institutions as "rules of the game" and organizations as "players in the game". Institutions are pervasive and influence any behavior that manifests any resemblance of regularity, including political behavior among political leaders, bureaucrats, and the citizenry itself. The strength and efficacy of institutions are conditioned by the nature and degree of divergence of interests in society. This makes the effect of institutions on economic performance largely an empirical matter.

Institutions can be economic, political or social in nature. The economic institutions determine the economic rules of the game, the degree of property rights enforcement, the set of contracts that can be written and enforced and the rules and regulations that determine the economic opportunities open to agents. In other words, institutions establish a stable structure to facilitate interactions, define and enforce property rights and determine the degree of competition by defining the terms of market entry (North, 1990; Coase, 1960). This helps in lowering both transaction costs and information costs by reducing uncertainty. Thus, the economic institutions shape the incentives structure for the key economic actors and hence influence investment decisions in physical and human capital and technology and the organization of production.

Political institutions, on the other hand, help in regulating political power and determine how this power changes hands. Political institutions may be crucial in resolving the conflicts of interest between multinational corporations and the host country government to maximize benefits and minimize negative externalities. This is so because the incentive to invest depends on the expected returns, which in turn depend on the protection of property rights (vertical relations between the state and the owners of private properties) and enforcement of contracts (the horizontal relations between the transacting parties). It is observed that the investors are reluctant to invest and risk their capital when property rights are weak and poorly protected, as under such circumstances the returns on investment may be appropriated by others. Besides, institutions also lay the foundation for the operation of the capital market and thereby conducive environment for an investment decision.

While the importance of an institutional framework for encouraging investment, especially through protection of property rights and enforcement of contracts, is well-established in the literature, there are debates on the regime of an institution that may be more appropriate in this regard. According to Jessup (1999), autocratic regimes provide the firms with better entry deals because of less executive constraints, thereby resulting in greater FDI inflows. In addition, authoritarian regimes lead to higher returns in developing countries (Oneal, 1994). In other words, the autocrats and the investors go together as autocratic leaders are merely interested in the benefits of the investment and they ensure it by shielding investors from public pressure and higher wages and offering them much lower capital taxation than would otherwise be expected (O'Donnell, 1978). Besides, since the autocrats have a smaller electorate, they have less distributional pressure and this allows them for greater variations in the economic policies (Haggard, 1990). Further, in some contexts, autocrats can confer and protect property rights.

Contrary to this, the proponents of democracy point out that such a system attracts more FDI because it has larger electorate, larger domestic coalitions, tends to be more stable and has greater scope for property rights violations (Feng, 2001; Pastor & Hilt, 1993; Pastor & Sung, 1995). Moreover, democracies have independent judiciaries and regular change in elected officials that strengthen property rights. Therefore, democracy should attract more investment inflows (Olson, 1993). According to Jensen (2003), democratic institutional constraints result in more policy stability and hence greater long-term FDI inflows. In other words, democracies can create an optimal investment environment (Li & Resnick, 2003).

Thus, institutional and political factors that affect the business environment can have a direct influence on FDI inflows. Generally, it is believed that better governance in the host country attracts more FDI inflow.

The available literature on institutional determinants of FDI suggests that good economic institutions like effective rule of law and strong IPR attract more FDI inflow into the host economy (Kaufmann & Kraay, 2002; Rodrik, Subramanian & Trebbi, 2004; Acemoglu, Johnson & Robinson, 2005). Against this, poor and weak institutional environment in terms of corruption and weak enforcement of contracts imposes an additional cost for the foreign investors and deter foreign investment in the host economy (Wei, 2000; Shleifer & Vishny, 1993). FDI has huge sunk costs. Hence it is very difficult for the foreign investors to make investment decisions. Foreign investors first assure and tie the long-term contract to reduce all types of uncertainty; therefore government stability and effective rule of law are especially important to attract higher FDI inflow in an economy (Naude & Krugell, 2007; Busse & Hefeker, 2007). According to World Bank (2003), the time spent by managers dealing with bureaucracy to obtain licenses and permits has a negative impact on FDI inflow across 69 countries. Some of the recent works have examined the role of institutional and political factors on capital flows from the developing to developing countries, known as South–South FDI. According to Aleksynska and Havrylchyk (2013), when MNCs from the emerging/developing (south) countries invest in countries with superior institutions, the institutional distance can be viewed as a motivating force as most of the emerging countries obtain new technologies, patents, IPR, trademarks and brands. MNCs believed that these ownership-specific advantages will be protected in a good institutional environment. They also found that FDI inflow is being averagely (not much) discouraged when emerging countries invest in countries with worse/incompetent institutions. The main reason behind this average impact is the investors or MNCs who had previous experience of weak/incompetent institutions may have a comparative advantage in investing in other emerging or developing economies that suffer from the weak institutions like ineffective rule of law, corruption and political instability. To take advantage of the previous experience with the corrupt environment, the investors from countries that would have high corruption and lack of enforcement of anti-corruption laws internalize their production with countries that have a similar corrupt environment (Cuervo-Cazura, 2006).

Habib and Zurawicki (2002) and Bénassy-Quéré, Coupet & Mayer (2007) used the concept of "psychic distance," which states that MNCs tend to enter a market where they found psychological closeness. Accordingly, they found that the larger institutional distance decreases FDI flows between the countries. Claessens and Van Horen (2008) found that the FDI flow in the banking industry is negatively impacted by the large distances in institutions. According to Darby, Desbordes & Wooton (2010), MNCs who have very little experience of imperfect institutions in the home economy are discouraged by institutional deficiencies abroad. Overall, the findings of these researches state that different investors have various motivation to invest into a particular location. They also find that weak institutions don't always deter the FDI inflow in host country; hence these countries should not always improve their quality in order to attract FDI.

Empirical works also examined that most of the increasing trend of south–south FDI is driven by natural resource-seeking purpose (Aleksynska & Havrylchyk, 2013). Countries that are endowed by natural resource availability have a very poor quality of institutions. Still there is significant FDI inflow into these countries. Most of the African countries don't have better institutions but recently most of the FDI from China has flowed into these African countries to take advantage of the natural resource availability. Asiedu (2006) found that large market size, natural resource endowment, macroeconomic stability, efficient legal system and a good investment framework promote FDI in African countries.

Country-specific institutional determinants of FDI inflow are different for different economies. According to Duanmu and Guney (2009), FDI outflow from China and India show important dissimilarities. Chinese FDI is encouraged by open economic regimes, depreciated host currency and better institutional environment, but these factors are not important for Indian FDI outflow in other countries. Mohamed and Sidiropoulos (2010) examined that the key determinants of FDI inflows in MENA countries are the size of the host economy, the government size, natural resources and the institutional variables.

Even though developing nations are taking significant steps to improve their investment climate, law and governance institutions and structures, human capital and infrastructure, and overall macro-economic management and services in order to boost FDI inflows, the countries in SAARC region still lag far behind other regions of the world in providing the necessary conditions for attracting foreign Investment. It is therefore important to understand the underlying factors, which are significantly linked with inflows of FDI to guide policy and institutional reforms and their effective implementation in the SAARC group of countries.

The role of these factors has been addressed by various scholars for different countries and regions in different time periods. However, the issue has not been addressed for the South Asian or the SAARC region. The current chapter tries to fulfill this lacuna by analyzing the role played by these institutional variables and their impact in reference to the SAARC region.

7.2. Data Sources and Methodology

The data for the various variables except for FDI used in this chapter are collected from the yearly publication of Heritage Foundation's "Index of Economic Freedom 2014." The data for the FDI inflows in the SAARC group of countries are collected from UNCTAD.

Due to unavailability of the continuous data, Maldives, Afghanistan and Bhutan have been dropped from the analysis.

In order to analyze the role of institutional variables in attracting FDI in the SAARC region, the present chapter covers 13 time periods (2000–2016) and five economies of the region. Time-series analysis for such a short period is not appropriate. The analysis based on simple cross-sectional data at the country level also becomes ineffective due to a limited number of observations (Baltagi, 2005). Since FDI is a dynamic process, panel data is more appropriate for a systematic and efficient analysis of various determinants (Dunning, 1993). Panel data method allows us to study dynamic as well as cross-sectional aspects of a problem. As it takes an average over the subjects, the statistics become more reliable and also we require fewer time-series observations to estimate dynamic patterns. A panel dataset possesses several other advantages over the cross-sectional or time-series dataset. Panel data model usually gives a larger number of data points, increasing the degrees of freedom, reducing the co-linearity among the explanatory variables and hence improving the efficiency of econometric estimates. It allows analysis of a number of important economic questions that cannot be tackled by cross-section or time-series data while becoming more informative.

In general, the panel data model can be written as

$$Y_{it} = \alpha_{it} + \sum_{k=1}^{k} \beta_{kit} X_{kit} + u_{it},$$

where i = 1, 2,..., N refers to cross-sectional units; t = 1, 2, 0,..., T refers to a given time period; k = 1, 2,..., K refers to number of explanatory variables.

Thus, Y_{it} represents the value of the dependent variable for the individual i and X_{kit} represents the values of the kth non-stochastic explanatory variables for the individual i at time t. The stochastic term u_{it}, assumed to have mean zero [E(u_{it}) = 0] and constant variance [$E(u_{it}^2) = \sigma^2 u . \beta_{kit}$], are unknown parameters of response coefficients. For the most general case, they can be different for different individuals in different time periods. β_{kit} is unknown parameters or response coefficients. The appropriate estimation procedure for the model depends upon whether the α_i are assumed to be random or fixed. The fixed assumption for α_i leads to fixed-effects (FE) model and seemingly unrelated regression (SUR) model, while the random assumption for α_i leads to error component model or random effects (RE) model and Swamy random coefficient model.

7.2.1. *Specification of panel data model (fixed effect or random effect)*

The model adopted for the present chapter is the one where varying intercept terms are assumed to capture differences in behavior over individuals and where the coefficients are assumed to be constant. This model, in general, can be written as

$$Y_{it} = \alpha_{it} + \sum_{k=1}^{k} \beta_k X_{kit} + u_{it}.$$

Thus, Y_{it} is the value of FDI inflow for the ith country at time t. X_{kit} are the value of such determinants as market size, trade openness and macroeconomic stability. The appropriate estimation procedure for this model depends upon whether α_i are assumed to be random or fixed. The fixed assumption for α_i leads to the FE model and SUR model, while the random assumption for α_i leads to a random effect model.

(1) Fixed Effect Model

The generalization of constant intercept and slope model for panel data is to introduce dummy variable to allow for the effects of those omitted variables that are specific to country cross-sectional units but stay constant over time and the effects that are specific to each time period but are the same for all cross-sectional units. In the present chapter, no time-specific effects are assumed and the focus is only on individual-specific effects. Thus, the value of dependent variable for the ith unit at time t. Y_{it}, depends on K exogenous variables ($X_{1it}, X_{2it}, ..., X_{kit}$) that differ across individuals at a given point in time t and also shows variation through time as well as on variables that are specific to the ith units and that stay constant over time.

(2) Random Effect Model

In the fixed effect model, the effects of omitted variables (individual-specific) are considered as fixed constants over time, whereas in the random effect model, the individual-specific effects are treated as random variables. Thus, α_i is assumed random. So in this case, α_i is distributed independently and identically with mean zero and constant variance. Here, the model is

$$Y_{it} = \mu + \underset{1*k}{\beta'} X_{1it} + v_{it},$$

$$v_{it} = \alpha_i + u_{it},$$

where α_i the individual-specific is time-invariant variable and u_{it} represents the effects of the omitted variables that vary with both individuals and time.

(3) Seemingly Unrelated Regression (SUR) Model

In several instances in an economy, one needs to estimate the various set of equations. This could be a set of demand equations, across different sectors, industries or regions. Other examples include the estimation of a trans log cost function along with the corresponding cost share equations. In these cases, Zellner's (1962) SUR approach is popular as it captures the efficiency of the studied system due to the correlation of the disturbances across equations. Applications of the SUR model with both time-series and cross-section data are too numerous to cite. There are two main motivations for the use of SUR in this context. The first one is to gain efficiency in estimation by combining information on differential equations. The second motivation is to impose and/or test restrictions that involve parameters in different equations.

7.3. Selection of Variables[1]

In order to understand the impact of institutional factors on FDI inflows, the present chapter captures various aspects of institutional effectiveness. The major variables selected for the analysis are business freedom, trade freedom, financial freedom, fiscal freedom and

---

[1] Adopted from Heritage Foundation (2013).

investment freedom. The business freedom is expected to reflect the efficiency of government regulation of business; trade freedom measures of the extent of tariff and nontariff barriers that affect imports and exports of goods and services. Financial freedom is expected to address the issues related to financial regulatory and independence enjoyed by foreign firms. Regulatory issues related to the fiscal mechanism is reflected fiscal freedom while investment freedom reflects the investment environment of the country. However, many of these aspects of institutions are inter-linked and thereby have simultaneous effects on FDI inflows. Details about these variables are explained below.

Business Freedom

Business freedom is an overall indicator of the efficiency of government regulation of business. The quantitative score is derived from an array of measurements of the ease of starting, operating and closing a business. The business freedom score for each country is a number between 0 and 100, with 100 indicating the freest business environment. The score is based on 10 factors, all weighted equally, using data from the World Bank's Doing Business report.

Trade Freedom

Trade freedom is a composite measure of the extent of tariff and non-tariff barriers that affect imports and exports of goods and services. The trade freedom score is based on two inputs:

- The trade-weighted average tariff rate
- Non-tariff barriers (NTBs)

Different imports entering a country can, and often do, face different tariffs. The weighted average tariff uses weights for each tariff based on the share of imports for each good. Weighted average tariffs are a purely quantitative measure and account for the calculation of the base trade freedom score using the following equation:

$$\text{Trade Freedom} = \left(\left(\frac{\text{Traiffmax} - \text{Tariffi}}{\text{Traiffmax} - \text{Tariffmin}} \right) * 100 \right) - \text{NTB}$$

where Trade Freedom represents the trade freedom in country i; Tariff max and Tariff min represent the upper and lower bounds for tariff rates (%); and Tariff represents the weighted average tariff rate (%) in country i. The minimum tariff is naturally 0%, and the upper bound was set as 50%. An NTB penalty is then subtracted from the base score. The penalty of 5, 10, 15 or 20 points are assigned according to the following scale.

Investment Freedom

In an economically free country, there would be no constraints on the flow of investment capital. Individuals and firms would be allowed to move their resources into and out of specific activities, both internally and across the country's borders, without restriction. Such an ideal country would receive a score of 100 on the investment freedom component of the index. In practice, however, most countries have a variety of restrictions on investment. Some have different rules for foreign and domestic investment; some restrict access to foreign exchange; some impose restrictions on payments, transfers and capital transactions; in some, certain industries are closed to foreign investment. The index evaluates a variety of regulatory restrictions that are typically imposed on investment.

Financial Freedom

Financial freedom is an indicator of banking efficiency as well as a measure of independence from government control and interference in the financial sector. State ownership of banks and other financial institutions such as insurers and capital markets reduces competition and generally lowers the level of access to credit. In an ideal banking and financing environment where a minimum level of government interference exists, independent central bank supervision and regulation of financial institutions are limited to enforcing contractual obligations and preventing fraud. Credit is allocated on market terms, and the government does not own financial institutions. Financial institutions provide various types of financial services to individuals and companies. Banks are free to extend credit, accept deposits and conduct operations in foreign currencies. Foreign financial institutions operate freely and are treated the same as domestic institutions.

Fiscal Freedom

The fiscal freedom component is a composite measure of the burden of taxes that reflects both marginal tax rates and the overall level of taxation, including direct and indirect taxes imposed by all levels of government, as a percentage of GDP. The component score is derived from three quantitative factors:

- The top marginal tax rate on individual income
- The top marginal tax rate on corporate income
- The total tax burden as a percentage of GDP

Each of these numerical variables is weighted equally as one-third of the component score. This equal weighting allows a country to achieve a score as high as 67 based on two of the factors even if it receives a score of 0 on the third. Fiscal freedom scores are calculated with a quadratic cost function to reflect the diminishing revenue returns from very high rates of taxation. The data for each factor are converted to a 100-point scale using the following equation:

$$\text{Fiscal Freedom}_{ij} = 100 - \alpha\,(\text{Factor}_{ij})2$$

where Fiscal Freedom$_{ij}$ represents the fiscal freedom in country i for factor j; Factor$_{ij}$ represents the value (a percentage expressed on a scale of 0 to 100) in country i for factor j; and α is a coefficient set equal to 0.03. The minimum score for each factor is zero, which is not represented in the printed equation but was utilized because it means that no single high tax burden will make the other two factors irrelevant.

7.4. Model Specification

$$FDI_{it} = \beta_0 + \beta_1 Fisfree_{it} + \beta_2 busfree_{it} + \beta_3 tradefree_{it} \\ + \beta_4 investment\ free_{it} + \beta_5 finfree_{it} + \mu_i + \varepsilon_{it}, \quad (1)$$

where t is the time period from $1,..., T$ (i.e., 2000–2016), i is the countries from $i,..., N$, fDI_i is the inflow of FDI in country i of SAARC region, *fisfree$_i$* is the Fiscal freedom of the country i, *busfree$_i$*

is the business freedom of the country i, *tradefree$_i$* is the trade free-dom of country i, *investment free$_i$* is the investment freedom of country i, *finfree$_i$* = financial freedom of country i, μ_i is the unobserv-able individual effects, ε_{it} is the error term.

7.4.1. *Results and discussion*

7.4.1.1. *The aggregate results*

For the present dataset, F and LM test results suggest the superiority of the panel model over the pooled model. Hausman test proves the FE model to be relatively efficient as compared to the RE model. Thus, the economic interpretation of the results is based on the FE model only. However, for the sake of comparison, the results of FE, RE and pooled data models are presented. Table 7.1 presents the results at the aggregate level considering five South Asian countries of the region and for 17 (year) time periods.

The results, by and large, follow the expected lines. To be spe-cific, the findings support the notion of a positive relationship between the selected variables and inflow of foreign investment flows. These factors represent the overall economic structure of an economy and seem to be powerful explanatory variables for FDI inflows.

Table 7.1:   Results of Panel Analysis

Variable	Pooled	Fixed Effects	Random Effects
Business freedom	0.242***	0.123***	0.453***
	(21.101)	(8.911)	(11.29)
Trade freedom	0.412***	0.243***	0.252***
	(19.103)	(5.741)	(17.26)
Investment freedom	0.742***	0.153***	0.213***
	(27.452)	(8.257)	(21.22)
Financial freedom	0.262***	0.122***	0.193***
	(29.208)	(6.211)	(19.55)
Fiscal freedom	0.352***	0.153***	0.273***
	(21.202)	(5.231)	(14.25)

7.4.1.2.   *Country-wise results*

The estimation process of the equation mentioned above starts with a SUR model by taking FDI inflow as a dependent variable and the major components of governance referred as FF for fiscal freedom, BF for business freedom, TF for trade freedom, IF for investment freedom and GF for governance freedom as independent variables. Table 7.2 summarizes the regression results. It is observed that the *F*-statistic is statistically significant and the value of adjusted R^2 is very high. Hence, the estimated model is statistically significant with very high explanatory power.

The Z-statistics for the individual coefficients computed on the basis of robust standard errors shows that the coefficient of BF and GF are statistically significant. However, while the coefficient of BF is positive, that of GF is negative. This means that business freedom in Bangladesh has a significant influence on variations in FDI inflows in Bangladesh. Higher business freedom raises FDI inflows into Bangladesh, whereas greater variations in it reduce the same. GF is negatively related to FDI inflow in Bangladesh.

However, the coefficient of FF, TF and IF are not statistically significant implying that fiscal freedom, trade freedom and investment freedom do not have any statistically significant impact on variations in FDI inflows in Bangladesh.

Table 7.2:   Regression Results of SUR Model: Bangladesh

Equation	Obs	Parms	RMSE	R^2	Chi^2	P
fdi_p	13	5	128.7874	0.7733	44.35	0
fdi_p	Coef.	Std. Err.	Z	P > z	[95% Conf. Interval]	
ff	16.91667	12.80954	1.32	0.187	−8.18958	42.02291
bf	16.5163	4.098183	4.03	0	8.484011	24.54859
tf	1.010617	2.897477	0.35	0.727	−4.66833	6.689568
if_r	4.492933	4.391733	1.02	0.306	−4.11471	13.10057
gf_r	−20.4275	6.862352	−2.98	0.003	−33.8774	−6.97751
_cons	−1198.46	1246.831	−0.96	0.336	−3642.2	1245.284

Table 7.3: Regression Results of SUR Model: India

Equation	Obs	Parms	RMSE	R^2	Chi^2	P
fdi_p	13	5	8711.645	0.6164	20.89	0.0008
fdi_p	Coef.	Std. Err.	Z	$P > z$	[95% Conf. Interval]	
ff	783.863	3147.574	0.25	0.803	−5385.27	6952.994
bf	712.6301	685.1357	1.04	0.298	−630.211	2055.471
tf	917.4264	288.1333	3.18	0.001	352.6955	1482.157
if_r	−19.2842	389.6388	−0.05	0.961	−782.962	744.3937
gf_r	−271.506	1224.05	−0.22	0.824	−2670.6	2127.588
_cons	−103149	292822.8	−0.35	0.725	−6770.72	470772.8

Overall the results for India (Table 7.3) indicate that all independent variables can explain 69% of the variation in FDI inflow in India. The coefficient of TF is statistically significant with a positive sign. This means that trade freedom, measured by the low level of tariff and non-tariff barriers, in India has a significant influence on variations in FDI inflows in India. This indicates that motivation behind FDI inflow in India is strategic asset-seeking as goods and services produced by the foreign firm are exported to another country. However, the coefficient of FF, BF, GF and IF are not statistically significant implying that fiscal freedom, business freedom, GF and investment freedom do not have any statistically significant impact on variations in FDI inflows in India. *F* statistics indicate that overall indicates are statistically significant.

FDI inflow into Pakistan (Table 7.4) is not affected by the qualitative factors as not a single independent variable from the model is statistically significant. The estimated model explains only 50% of the variation in the dependent variable. Overall results are statistically significant as explained by the *F* statistics as the probability of *F* statistics is less than *F* statistics.

The result from the SUR model indicates that the estimated model explains 94% variation in FDI inflow to Nepal (Table 7.5).

Table 7.4:   Regression Results of SUR Model: Pakistan

Equation	Obs	Parms	RMSE	R^2	Chi^2	P
fdi_p	13.0	5.0	1290.0	0.5	11.9	0.0
FDI_p	Coef.	Std. Err.	Z	P > z	[95% Conf. interval	
ff	−48.8	85.0	−0.6	0.6	−215.4	117.7
bf	97.1	86.0	1.1	0.3	−71.5	265.7
tf	133.5	74.5	1.8	0.1	−12.5	279.4
if_r	92.7	52.5	1.8	0.1	−10.2	195.7
gf_r	−41.0	60.6	−0.7	0.5	−159.7	77.7
_cons	−10996.1	10257.6	−1.1	0.3	−31100.7	9108.6

Table 7.5:   Regression Results of SUR Model: Nepal

Equation	Obs	Parms	RMSE	R^2	Chi^2	P
FDI_p	13	5	8.511905	0.9438	364.72	0
FDI_p	Coef.	Std. Err.	Z	P > z	[95% Conf. Interval]	
ff	−0.189541	2.778226	−0.07	0.946	−5.634764	5.255683
bf	−0.611454	0.843245	−0.73	0.468	−2.264185	1.041276
tf	0.2719719	0.678298	0.4	0.688	−1.057467	1.601411
if_r	−3.984245	0.295347	−13.49	0	−4.563114	−3.40538
gf_r	5.408947	8.805603	0.61	0.539	−11.84972	22.66761
_cons						

Investment freedom has a positive impact on FDI inflow in Nepal. The coefficient of FF, BF, TF, and GF are not statistically significant implying that fiscal freedom, business freedom, trade freedom and government freedom do not have any statistically significant impact on variations in FDI inflows in Nepal.

The result from the SUR model indicates that the estimated model explains 60% variation in FDI inflow to Sri Lanka (Table 7.6). Independent variables for Sri Lanka have an impact similar to those of Nepal. Investment freedom has a positive impact on FDI inflow in Sri Lanka. The coefficient of FF, BF, TF and GF are not statistically

Table 7.6:   Regression Results of SUR Model: Sri Lanka

Equation	Obs	Parms	RMSE	R^2	Chi^2	P
fdi_p	13	5	160.3685	0.6076	20.13	0.0012
fdi_p	Coef.	Std. Err.	Z	$P > z$	[95% Conf. Interval]	
ff	−9.361647	23.6773	−0.4	0.693	−55.76831	37.04502
bf	−12.57229	35.1383	−0.36	0.72	−81.44209	56.29751
tf	41.90829	26.04907	1.61	0.108	−9.146955	92.96354
if_r	−19.96129	8.560454	−2.33	0.02	−36.73947	−3.18311
gf_r	4.719067	12.20532	0.39	0.699	−19.20291	28.64105
_cons	−400.4532	2985.302	−0.13	0.893	−6251.538	5450.631

significant implying that fiscal freedom, business freedom, trade freedom and government freedom do not have any statistically significant impact on variations in FDI inflows in Nepal.

7.5. Conclusion

Apart from liberal FDI policy, there are some other related policy variables that also play a vital role in attracting FDI in a country. The current chapter made an attempt to analyze some of these important variables in the context of SAARC countries. The variables selected for the analysis were business freedom, trade freedom, investment freedom, financial freedom and fiscal freedom. To analyze these variables, the SUR model was used. SUR model captures the efficiency in the variables due to the correlation of the disturbances across equations. The SUR model can be applied with both time-series and cross-section data.

In the case of Bangladesh, only business freedom has a significant influence on variations in FDI inflows in Bangladesh. This implies that fiscal freedom, trade freedom and investment freedom do not have any statistically significant impact on variations in FDI inflows in Bangladesh.

In the case of India, trade freedom, which is measured by a low level of tariff and non-tariff barriers, is found to have a significant influence on variations in FDI inflows in India. This reflects the motivation behind FDI inflows in India are strategic asset-seeking as goods and services produce by the foreign firm are exported to another country. However, the coefficient of FF, BF, GF and IF are not statistically significant implying that fiscal freedom, business freedom, GF and investment freedom do not have any statistically significant impact on variations in FDI inflows in India.

None of the selected variables have any impact on the inflow of FDI in Pakistan. In the case of Nepal, Investment freedom has a positive impact on FDI inflow in Nepal. The result of Nepal indicates that fiscal freedom, business freedom, trade freedom and government freedom do not have any statistically significant impact on variations in FDI inflows. Similar results were also noticed in the case of Sri Lanka.

It can be concluded from the above that the different policy variables have played a major role in attracting FDI inflows in different SAARC countries. But, what is pertinent to note that the policy changes that lead to increasing in various freedom lead to larger FDI inflows.

References

Acemoglu, D., Johnson, S., & Robinson, J. A. (2005). Institutions as a Fundamental Cause of Long-Run Growth. *Handbook of Economic Growth*, 1, 385–472.

Aleksynska, M., & Havrylchyk, O. (2013). FDI from the South: The Role of Institutional Distance and Natural Resources. *European Journal of Political Economy*, 29, 38–53.

Asiedu, E. (2006). Foreign Direct Investment in Africa: The Role of Natural Resources, Market Size, Government Policy, Institutions, and Political Instability. *The World Economy*, 29(1), 63–77.

Baltagi, (2005). *Econometric Analysis of Panel Data,* New York: Wiley.

Bénassy-Quéré, A., Coupet, M., & Mayer, T. (2007). Institutional Determinants of Foreign Direct Investment. *The World Economy*, 30(5), 764–782.

Busse, M., & Hefeker, C. (2007). Political Risk, Institutions and Foreign Direct Investment. *European Journal of Political Economy*, 23(2), 397–415.

Claessens, S., Horen, V. N. (2008). Location Decisions of Foreign Banks and Institutional Competitive Advantage, DNB Working Papers, 172.

Coase, R. H. (1960). Problem of Social Cost. *Journal of Law and Economics*, 3, 1–44.

Cuervo-Cazurra, A. (2006). Who Cares about Corruption? *Journal of International Business Studies*, 37(6), 807–822.

Darby, J., Desbordes, R., & Wooton, I. (2010). Does Public Governance Always Matter? How Experience of Poor Institutional Quality Influences FDI to the South: CESIFO Working Paper: Trade Policy.

Duanmu, J.-L., & Guney, Y. (2009). A Panel Data Analysis of Locational Determinants of Chinese and Indian Outward Foreign Direct Investment. *Journal of Asia Business Studies*, 3(2), 1–15.

Dunning, T. (1993). Accurate Methods for the Statistics of Surprise and Coincidence. *Computational Linguistics*, 19(1), 61–74.

Feng, Y. (2001). Political Freedom, Political Instability, and Policy Uncertainty: A Study of Political Institutions and Private Investment in Developing Countries. *International Studies Quarterly*, 45(2), 271–294.

Greif, A. (2006). *Institutions and the Path to the Modern Economy: Lessons from Medieval Trade*. Cambridge University Press, UK.

Habib, M., & Zurawicki, L. (2002). Corruption and Foreign Direct Investment. *Journal of International Business Studies*, 33(2), 291–307.

Haggard, S. (1990). *Pathways from the Periphery: The Politics of Growth in the Newly Industrializing Countries*. Cornell University Press.

Heritage Foundation (2013). *Index of Economic Freedom*, Heritage Foundation, USA.

Jensen, N. M. (2003). Democratic Governance and Multinational Corporations: Political Regimes and Inflows of Foreign Direct Investment. *International organization*, 57(03), 587–616.

Jessup, D. (1999). Dollars and Democracy: Developing Country Democracies Declining Share of Trade and Investment Markets. *New Economy Information Services*. Institute for Agriculture and Trade Policy, Washington DC.

Kaufmann, D., & Kraay, A. (2002). Growth without Governance, World Bank Policy Research Working Paper 2928.

Li, Q., & Resnick, A. (2003). Reversal of Fortunes: Democratic Institutions and Foreign Direct Investment Inflows to Developing Countries, *International Organization*, 57(01), 175–211.

Mohamed, S. E., & Sidiropoulos, M. G. (2010). Another Look at the Determinants of Foreign Direct Investment in Mena Countries: An Empirical Investigation. *Journal of Economic Development*, 35(2), 75–95.

Naudé, W., & Krugell, W. (2007). Investigating Geography and Institutions as Determinants of Foreign Direct Investment in Africa using Panel Data. *Applied Economics*, 39(10), 1223–1233.

North, D. C. (1990). *Institutions, Institutional Change, and Economic Performance*, Cambridge University Press, UK.

O'donnell, G. (1978). Reflections on the Patterns of Change in the Bureaucratic-Authoritarian State. *Latin American Research Review*, 13(1), 3–38.

Olson, M. (1993). Dictatorship, Democracy, and Development. *American Political Science Review*, 87(03), 567–576.

Oneal, J. R. (1994). The Affinity of Foreign Investors for Authoritarian Regimes. *Political Research Quarterly*, 47(3), 565–588.

Pastor Jr, M., & Hilt, E. (1993). Private Investment and Democracy in Latin America. *World Development*, 21(4), 489–507

Pastor Jr, M., & Sung, J. H. (1995). Private Investment and Democracy in the Developing World. *Journal of Economic Issues*, 29(1), 223–243.

Rodrik, D., Subramanian, A., & Trebbi, F. (2004). Institutions Rule The Primacy of Institutions over Geography and Integration in Economic Development. *Journal of Economic Growth*, 9(2), 131–165.

Shleifer, A., Vishny, W. R. (1993). Corruption. *Quarterly Journal of Economics*, 108(3), 599–617.

Wei, S.-J. (2000). How Taxing is Corruption on International Investors? *Review of Economics and Statistics*, 82(1), 1–11.

World Bank (2003). Trade, Investment, and Development in the Middle East and North Africa: Engaging with the World, World Bank, Washington, D.C.

Zellner, A. (1962). An Efficient Method of Estimating Seemingly Unrelated Regressions and Tests for Aggregation Bias. *Journal of the American Statistical Association*, 57(298), 348–368.

Chapter 8

Summary and Conclusion

The prime intention of the book is to throw light on the trade and investment scenario in SAARC countries. The book provides an overview of the current trend of trade and FDI inflows in the region for from various parts of the world. The book attempted to investigate the relationship between trade and FDI in the SAARC region. The role of investment policy and institutional variables in attracting FDI in the region has also been analyzed. The book also looked into the various obstacles faced by the corporate sector in doing business in these countries after entering them through the foreign investment route. The variables that facilitate the doing business and the variables that pose threat to the business are discussed in detail in the book. It is in this context the book developed a framework for analyzing the role of FDI in the SAARC region both at the regional level as a whole and individual country level. The main findings of the book for each of the chapters are summarized in this chapter.

8.1. Major Findings of the Book

In Chapter 1, the objectives and hypothesis of the research were presented.

In Chapter 2, the existing theories of international investment and review of empirical studies were described.

In Chapter 3, the trend of the trade and foreign direct investment inflows for the selected SAARC countries were analyzed. The chapter also analyzed the intra-regional trend of trade and investment flows for a few of the selected countries.

In the case of FDI in Bangladesh, sectors like agro-based industry, chemicals, textiles and engineering was the major recipients. Here, the major investing countries were UAE, Saudi Arabia and the UK. In the case of trade for Bangladesh, the total trade value, which was only $13,546.1 million in 2000, has increased to $29,903.4 million in 2012. This represents a rate of more than 100% increase during this time period. The maximum amount of trade occurred in 2011. The total value of the trade in that year was $32,607 million. The results found apparel and clothing accessories were the most exported items from Bangladesh. Bangladesh exported apparel and clothing worth $9936 million in 2011. The apparel and clothing sector had also attracted the highest amount of FDI for Bangladesh. Cotton, nuclear reactors and animal/vegetable fats were found to be major importing items of Bangladesh.

Bhutan, the smallest economy of the region, could not attract much FDI during the period selected for our book. However, in 2006, an investment of $72 million was made in Bhutan by Ferro Silicon from India. This was the highest amount of FDI received by Bhutan in our reference period. The major investments in Bhutan have come from India, followed by Germany and Singapore. Sector-wise, an unprecedented 60% investment is concentrated in a single power project, namely, Dagachhu Hydro Power Corporation Ltd., promoted by the Asian Development Bank. The first public–private partnership (PPP) project in Bhutan was realized with Druk Green Power Corporation (DGPC), Tata Power and the National Pension Fund as joint venture partners.

Both export and import values of Bhutan have increased tremendously in our reference period. The total trade value, which was only $166.5 million in 2000, has increased to $1071 million in 2012. There was a tenfold increase in the volume of the trade. The highest volume of trade took place in 2011. The values of trade in that year were $1637 million. The study finds that iron and steel was the top exporting product in that year. It was followed by electrical machinery, salt and copper, while nuclear reactors and boilers were the top importing goods in 2011.

Countries like Mauritius, Singapore, the United States and the UK were the major investors in India. Out of the total FDI inflow in India, 42% has come from Mauritius while the share of United States and UK was 7% and 5%, respectively, in that year. Service sector (both financial and non-financial) has attracted the highest amount of FDI, followed by computer and telecommunication services. Service sector attracted 21% of the total investment while two other major sectors have managed to attract 8% of the FDI each in the same time period.

The trade volume of India continuously increased from 2000 to 2008. But in 2009 the trade volume decreased to $424,673.0 million from $473,600.9 million in 2008. The economic downturn in the United States and EU has affected India's export. Further, the depreciation in the Indian currency has increased the import value of India. In 2011, mineral fuels were the top exporting good of India. India exported more than $56,556 million worth of mineral fuels in that year. Mineral fuels were followed by natural/cultured pearls. The export value for this product in that particular year was more than $50,015 million.

India imported mineral fuels worth more than $157,356 million in 2011. India being an oil-deficit country imports more than two-thirds of its oil requirement. Apart from mineral fuels, the other major items in the import basket of India are natural/cultured pearls, nuclear reactors, electrical machinery, etc. Like mineral fuel, India also imports raw pearls and diamonds and other precious metals and exports it after value addition.

In the case of Nepal, the majority of the FDI has been made in the various manufacturing sector. It was followed by services and tourism industry including hotel and restaurants. Among the manufacturing industries, the textile sector including readymade garments, chemicals, and plastic, food, beverage, tobacco sector, fabricated metal sectorare the main industries that have attracted foreign investment. Around 10% in terms of total FDI value has gone into the textile sector. Hotels and restaurants received FDI of around 40%, while electricity attracted FDI of 21% and services received 15%.

The trade data of Nepal shows the value of trade, which was only $2298 million in 2000, has increased to $6572.7 million in 2011. The data reveals that iron and steel was the most exported product from Nepal in 2011. Nepal exported iron and steel worth of $117 million, which was top in the list while carpets and other textile floor materials were second in the list. Nepal imported mineral fuels worth more than $1225 million. Nepal has imported iron and steel worth of $493 million in 2011.

It is observed from the results that the infrastructure sector (telecom, power generation) and manufacturing sector (textile, chemicals, rubber) are among the major recipients of FDI in Sri Lanka. Among the South Asian investors, India is the biggest investor. It is also observed that Indian investment in Sri Lanka has mainly gone in the areas like margarine, Vanaspati ghee, steel products, PVC, furniture, herbal products, electric items, copper and metals.

Having discussed the trend Chapter 3, in Chapter 4, we captured the trade and investment relationship in the SAARC region. In this chapter, the gravity model was used to test the complementary or substitution relationship between trade and FDI in SAARC. The analysis was carried out for the top five investing countries in the SAARC nations excluding Afghanistan, Maldives and Bhutan. The results found both complementary and supplementary relationship between trade and FDI in all the SAARC group of countries. The results show a complementary relationship for all the selected countries with exception of Sri Lanka. India is a bigger market in size, and with developed infrastructure and low wage rate, it was able to attract the highest amount of FDI in the region. For exports of Bangladesh, the proposition of gravity model was not found to be applicable while it was true in case of imports. Similarly, Indian exports rejected the gravity model while it was accepted in the case of imports. The same result was also found in the case of Pakistan where exports rejected the gravity model but it was accepted by imports. Both exports and imports of Nepal and Sri Lanka confirmed the assumption that longer distance reduces trade. The chapter concluded with the finding that the relationship between trade and investment mainly depends upon the types of FDI flows and not on its volume.

In Chapter 5, we analyzed whether trade leads to a higher volume of FDI inflows or FDI is enhancing the trade volume. The chapter employs the gravity model to investigate this relationship — a complementary relationship for all the selected countries with exception of Sri Lanka. The result finds that during 2000–2016, an inflow of FDI in the region through various MNCs has helped to increase the trade, i.e., both exports and imports, from the region. For all the selected countries, both the trade values and FDI inflows have increased substantially.

The investigation to understand the relationship between trade and FDI was further expanded in Chapter 6 using a different methodology referred to as the Granger-causality modem. The chapter investigated if any causal relation exists between trade and FDI in the SAARC countries. The Granger causality method was employed to analyze the relationship for the time period from 1980 to 2012. The findings indicate that the series is stationary in the levels with two structural breaks. To test the causality relationship among the variables, Granger causality test based on the VAR model is applied. As per the findings, it is clear that there is no causal relationship between FDI and trade in the SAARC region. That is, neither trade is leading to higher FDI inflows nor high FDI inflows are enhancing the trade volume. Although theory states that greater inflow of FDI will lead to greater trade. This is not so in the case of SAARC countries. One possible reason for this may be that the conditions in the SAARC region, in general, are not conducive for larger FDI flows.

Apart from liberal FDI policy, there are some other related policy variables that also play a vital role in attracting FDI in a country. Chapter 7 made an attempt to analyze some of those important variables in the context of SAARC countries. The variables selected for the analysis were business freedom, trade freedom, investment freedom, financial freedom, and fiscal freedom. To analyze these variables the SUR model was used. SUR model captures the efficiency in the variables due to the correlation of the disturbances across equations. The SUR model can be applied with both time-series and cross-section data.

In the case of Bangladesh, only business freedom has a significant influence on variations in FDI inflows in Bangladesh. Other selected variables like fiscal freedom, trade freedom and investment freedom do not have any statistically significant impact on variations in FDI inflows in Bangladesh. In the case of India, trade freedom is found to have a significant influence on variations in FDI inflows in India. This reflects the motivation behind FDI inflows in India are strategic asset-seeking as goods and services produced by the foreign firm are exported to another country. However, the coefficient of FF, BF, GF and IF are not statistically significant implying that fiscal freedom, business freedom, GF and investment freedom do not have any statistically significant impact on variations in FDI inflows in India.

None of the selected variables have any impact on the inflow of FDI in Pakistan. In the case of Nepal, only investment freedom was found to have a positive impact on FDI inflow. Similar results were also noticed in the case of Sri Lanka.

From this book, that the following conclusions can be made:

- The formation of SAARC has not led to a significant increase in trade and investment in the SAARC group of countries.
- The intra-regional trade and investment flows have grown more rapidly than inter-regional trade and investment flows.
- Changes in some of the policy variables have encouraged investment flows to SAARC countries. Further, except for India, the FDI policy, in general, has not been a success in the majority of the SAARC countries.

Based on the results, the book recommends the following policy changes.

8.2. Policy Recommendations

The issues of infrastructural constraint, political instability and sometimes strained diplomatic relationships become deterrents for the process to move forward in case of bilateral trade and investment in the region. To integrate South Asia in a more pragmatic manner, progressive policies are required to reflect a balanced view related to security, trust and economic cooperation. As culturally nations are closely linked, more people-to-people contact, exchange of scholars and artists play a very important role for further integration along with trade fairs and business to business meeting. Countries are engaged in these initiatives to some extent but perhaps more effort is required for political decision-making. The yearly meeting of heads of state and high-ranking officials of the SAARC nations is also necessary.

FDI policies are more or less liberal in these countries. However, the business sector finds several gaps in the post-entry stages, especially in associated laws in conducting business in the countries. Labor laws, equity transfer, trading permits, profit repatriation regulation, visa, work permits, power crisis, infrastructural bottlenecks and lack of transparency in land title have been identified as major areas where companies face difficulties. Interpretation of several laws and regulation also require clarity. Capacity development is necessary to equip government officers to handle these issues. The approval process for FDI is quite fast in the selected countries but in post-entry situation, decision on companies' request/application on business-related issues takes an unusually long time. Speediness and transparency in government procedure are highlighted among the most warranted requirements by companies.

The region can gain immensely from the investment outflow and inflow but internal stability and removal of bottlenecks in the post-entry stage will be a challenge for the host country. There are countries like Nepal, Bhutan and Bangladesh where the outflow is not allowed, but there is a sizeable proportion of business groups waiting to invest locally in the region to take advantages for their own units and of the region. It may be worthwhile to consider the option of doing a phased opening only within South Asia. Such initiatives may help the country, company and the region. The region's biggest challenge, however, will continue to be the infrastructure sector, which is challenging in most cases. This sector can itself be a conduit for FDI.

Index

CPSIA information can be obtained
at www.ICGtesting.com
Printed in the USA
JSHW021743240919
1588JS00002B/2

9 789811 206566